SENSITIVITY AND AWARENESS

A GUIDE FOR DEVELOPING
UNDERSTANDING AMONG CHILDREN

By
Norma H. McPhee

Kindergarten materials by
Paddy C. Favazza, Ed.D.

Sensitivity Experiences by
Eleanore Grater Lewis

JASON & NORDIC PUBLISHERS
HOLLIDAYSBURG, PENNSYLVANIA

TURTLE BOOKS USED IN THIS STUDY

COOKIE by Linda Kneeland
BUDDY'S SHADOW by Shirley Becker
WHEN I GROW UP by Candri Hodges
THE NIGHT SEARCH by Kate Chamberlin

The following by Nan Holcomb
DANNY AND THE MERRY-GO-ROUND
ANDY FINDS A TURTLE
HOW ABOUT A HUG
PATRICK AND EMMA LOU
A SMILE FROM ANDY
ANDY OPENS WIDE
SARAH'S SURPRISE
FAIR AND SQUARE

Illustrations are taken from some of the TURTLE BOOKS listed above.

Copyright © 1998   by JASON & NORDIC PUBLISHERS
All rights reserved. No part of this book may be reproduced in
any form without permission from the publisher.

Library of Congress Cataloging-in-Publication Data

McPhee, Norma.
        Sensitivity and Awareness: a guide for developing understanding among children /
by Norma H. McPhee : kindergarten materials by Paddy C. Favazza : sensitivity
experiences by Eleanore Grater Lewis.- 3rd ed.
            p. cm.
        ISBN 0-944727-34-4 (paper)
        Includes bibliographical references (p.).
        1. Handicapped children--Education (Preschool-Middle school) 2. Empathy--Study
and teaching 3. Storytelling. 4. Group relations training. 5. Education, Preschool-
Middle school--Activity programs. I. Favazza, Paddy C.1954- . II. Lewis, Eleanore
Grater. III. Title.
LC4019.2.M33 1998
371.9'0472--dc21   97-42840
                                                                CIP

Printed in the United States of America

ISBN 0-944727-34-4

For all the children,

Moms, Dads, Grandpas and Grandmas

who have ever heard,

"Hey, what's the matter with that kid?"

TABLE OF CONTENTS

ABOUT THE AUTHORS AND CONTRIBUTORS

Norma H. McPhee is an author and teacher. She has had fourteen books published for children and young adults as well as several plays, curriculum materials, articles, short stories and photo essays for a variety of ages and with several publishing houses. She has taught music education and worked in music therapy with pre-school through young adult age groups in special education situations as well as music education in several elementary and junior high schools.

Mrs. McPhee graduated from State University of New York at Fredonia with a degree in music education. She has done extensive graduate study at SUNY and Immaculata College in Malvern, Pennsylvania. Since 1986 she has led numerous workshops, retreats, and made Head Start presentations in public schools and churches throughout the Eastern United States promoting understanding and awareness among non-disabled children through adults. She has been featured in numerous newspaper articles and made television appearances on behalf of the Easter Seal Society and to promote disability awareness programs. In 1988, after struggling to interest other publishers in publishing books for young children with disabilities, she established Jason & Nordic Publishers, becoming a pioneer in this newly emerging field.

Dr. Paddy C. Favazza has worked in the field of special education for 20 years teaching young children with disabilities, preparing teachers to work with children with disabilities, and conducting research. She received her doctorate from George Peabody College at Vanderbilt University and is currently a professor in Early Childhood Special Education at The University of Memphis. Her research activities include promoting the social relationships between young children with and without disabilities.

Dr. Favazza's research includes the development of a reliable measure of acceptance of young children with disabilities (the Acceptance Scale for Kindergartners - Revised (ASK-R), and effective strategies for promoting acceptance of children with disabilities. In addition, she provides training materials and workshops that enable teachers to create more accepting early childhood environments. Her work has been presented at regional, national and international levels and is currently being utilized in the United States, Korea and South Africa.

Eleanore Grater Lewis is Associate Director of the New England Resource Access Project for Disabilities Services at Educational Development Center (EDC) Inc. of Newton, Massachusetts.

Mrs. Lewis has her Master's Degree in Early Childhood Education and has taught in both public and private settings. She directed the Lexington Nursery and Kindergarten School, a program for children with and without special needs. For seventeen years she was involved in a national competency based system for credentialing caregivers in the field of Early Childhood. She teaches at several local colleges, is a popular speaker at conferences and has presented workshops on a wide variety of topics.

In recognition for her work in pioneering integrated settings for children with special needs, she was elected to the Alumni Hall of Fame of Hunter College of the City University of New York.

Judy Foil, recently named as a member of the Louisiana State Planning Council for Developmental Disabilities, has long been a community activist, particularly in the field of mental retardation. She was instrumental in the creation of the Down Syndrome Center and on the original board of the Down syndrome Awareness Group. Her interest in educating nondisabled students about their disabled classmates led to the founding of **Be A Friend.** This organization has sponsored awareness programs in the elementary schools each fall since 1990. In 1992 Mrs. Foil was awarded the J.C. Penney Golden Rule Award for this program.

She wrote the story "Peer Buddies: I Can Help" when she found no other story that taught the particular lesson needed on inclusion.

Kathy Kennedy Tapp, has written several children's novels, including *Smoke from the Chimney* and *Den 4 Meets the Jinx.* She has taught creative writing at school, workshops and conferences throughout the Midwest. Her husband, Ken, was an orientation and mobility teacher for many years at the Wisconsin School for the Visually Handicapped and is now an outreach consultant. It was watching some of his mobility lessons with his students that gave Kathy the idea for "Polka Dot Birthday Map."

To contact the authors:
  Norma McPhee: e-mail, turtlbks@nb.net
                    website:www.nb.net/~turtlbks
  Paddy Favazza: e-mail, Favazza.Paddy@COE.Memphis.EDU
    web site:http://www.coe.memphis.edu/coe/ICL/FAVAZZA/favazza1.html
  Eleanore Grater Lewis: e-mail, Eleanore@edc.org

  Kathy Kennedy Tapp: e-mail, kathtapp@aol.com

  Judy Foil: c/o Jason & Nordic Publisher's, P.O. Box 441
                    Hollidaysburg, PA 16648

INTRODUCTION

A woman who had lived for many years in an area of the country where there are many people of all ages, races, nationalities and varying physical and mental disabilities, picked up a copy of A SMILE FROM ANDY. When she finished reading the book, she looked at the person she was with and said, "My, I never knew they wanted people to notice them."

After the realization comes to us that these people who are different in many ways from some of us, have similar needs and feelings, another problem presents itself.

What do we do?
How do we meet the needs?
How do we approach Andy or Danny or Sarah?
Why do we feel awkward and unsure about reaching out?

How do we prepare our children before they meet a child who has a disability so that child is not hurt emotionally and the nondisabled child is labeled insensitive?

We find a way to approach the problem in a non-threatening way.

And that brings us to this guide.

ABOUT THE GUIDE

This guide is planned for use by classroom teachers, librarians or consultants concerned with improving relationships among disabled and non-disabled children within the school. The materials provided should fit within a one hour session. Each session is based on one of the Turtle Books written for children with disabilities. It would be suitable for use by parents, members of advocacy groups and other volunteer presenters.

Included are:

- brief facts needed to present background material about disabilities
- suggested questions to help lead group discussion
- 'how-tos' to help carry out activities with the group to reinforce the learnings
- a 'to-be-copied' page for each session as a take home activity paper

The material is designed to provide an opportunity to explore feelings, ask and answer questions about disabilities and the circumstances causing various disabilities. Sometimes children are fearful that they may develop a disability. These sessions can address these fears as the leader presents facts and encourages questions.

To emphasize similarities:

Each session explores the similarities between the child with the disability and children who are non-disabled. Andy wanted to be noticed. He wanted to have people talk to him. Buddy wanted a friend. Kevin wanted to play and win or lose on his own--fair and square! Jimmy wanted to know what he could be when he grew up. These are situations that face most children at some time in growing up. (This is discussed more completely in "The Person Comes First"). Children with disabilities must cope with these everyday challenges. Children with disabilities are real kids with real problems just like any other children.

This brings us to our goal for this program of sensitivity and awareness.

GOAL: As persons come to see the similarities and the challenges we share, they will become more understanding and caring toward persons with disabilities.

THE PERSON COMES FIRST

Whatever attributes each of us are born with are normal for us. If we have red hair and blue eyes, we may not always be pleased with red hair and blue eyes, but they are normal for us. If Mary is born with short genes and remains the shortest girl in the class, she may wish to be tall, but she is short. And short is, for Mary, normal. If, from birth, Andy has cerebral palsy, Andy has only known life with cerebral palsy. For Andy that is normal. Short people, red haired people, people who have Down syndrome, cerebral palsy or hearing and speech disabilities are people who need friendship, attention, understanding just as we all do.

They are real people.

Having a disability doesn't make an individual noble, heroic, patient, or saintly. Children who have disabilities have temper tantrums, dislike certain foods or colors, refuse to cooperate as frequently as they would if they were nondisabled. They have all the basic needs for love, acceptance, approval that we all have.

They are real people.

As we think and speak about persons with disabilities, we keep the person first. In your thinking, put the person first, not the disability. Emphasize abilities, not limitations. For example, say, "Jane uses a walker or wheelchair," instead of "Jane is confined to her wheelchair." Relegate the disability to the background of your mind. If the disability is important to the conversation or the action, treat it matter-of-factly. Keep in mind that it is normal for that person to have that condition.

'Person first' is the single most important thought to keep in mind.

The boy who has....
The girl who is....

They are real people with real problems, real needs and real feelings... just like you and just like me.

WHAT ARE DISABILITIES?

General Background Material

WHAT IS A DISABILITY?

A disability is a functional limitation that interferes with a person's ability to move independently, communicate verbally, to hear, to see, to learn. It may refer to a physical, mental or sensory condition.

¤ Physical limitations might include a limited ability to walk, talk, use hands and arms, hold up the head, sit up, control bladder and bowels or may be a seizure disorder.

¤ Mental limitations may include limited ability to remember, to learn traditional school subjects, to learn social and vocational skills.

¤ Sensory limitations may include visual impairment, hearing impairment.

HOW DO PEOPLE BECOME DISABLED?

¤ Some conditions happen before a baby is born. Two of the most common pre-birth conditions are Down syndrome and spina bifida.

¤ Some disabilities may occur at birth because a baby is born too early (premature) or there may be birth complications that cause lack of oxygen reaching the brain for too long a period of time.

¤ Some may be caused early in life from injury to the head, from something that interferes with breathing, from disease or infection.

¤ A few conditions may be inherited.

¤ Some disabilities occur later in childhood as a result of accidents causing head or spinal cord injuries. These may be caused by everyday activities.

NOTES ON SPECIFIC DISABILITIES

DOWN SYNDROME

Down syndrome gets its name from Dr. John Langdon-Downs who studied many babies having the characteristics we associate with Down syndrome today.

¤ Down syndrome is a chromosomal disorder which usually causes physical and mental developmental delays. The exact cause and prevention is unknown.

¤ Down syndrome is the leading cause of mental retardation in the world. It is not related to racial nor ethnic origins and is found in all socio-economic groups. In the United States one child is born with Down syndrome in every 800 - 1100 live births with about 4000 born each year.

¤ There is a wide variation in mental abilities, behavior and physical development in individuals with Down syndrome.

¤ Many, (approximately one third) have heart defects or other congenital defects of the gastro-intestinal tract. Most of these defects can now be corrected by surgery.

¤ Loving home care, early intervention, special education, and understanding, positive attitudes of associates are very important for developing maximum potential in children with Down syndrome.

¤ Down syndrome is not contagious.

SPINA BIFIDA

Spina bifida is the #1 disabling birth defect. Spina bifida or "open spine" affects approximately 1 out of every 1000 newborns in the United States. Spina bifida is a defect in the spinal column resulting from the failure of the spine to close during the first month of pregnancy.

¤ Spina bifida may be caused by diet deficiency and/or genetic factors. Recent findings indicate a connection between folic acid deficiency and spina bifida.

¤ Spina bifida may cause varying degrees of paralysis, loss of feeling in lower body, loss of bowel and bladder control. It is often accompanied by hydrocephalus (accumulation of fluid in the brain).

¤ Spina bifida is not contagious.

Thanks to revolutionary surgical techniques and mechanical aids most children born with spina bifida grow to adulthood, live a normal life span and live full, productive lives.

CEREBRAL PALSY

Cerebral palsy is a group of disabling conditions that result from damage to the central nervous system. It can be severe with resulting inability to control most body movements. Or it may be mild, slightly affecting a hand, foot or speech. It is not hereditary, contagious, progressive or a primary cause of death.

CEREBRAL PALSY CAN HAPPEN BEFORE, DURING OR AFTER BIRTH

Damage to the brain before or during birth may be caused by:

¤ Mother's illness. Certain viral diseases such as German measles can seriously affect the fetus.

¤ Complications in pregnancy and/or labor may deprive the brain of oxygen.

¤ Premature birth. Breathing problems may deprive the brain of oxygen.

Damage to the brain early in life may be the result of:

¤ Accidental injury from a fall or blow to the head.

¤ Lead poisoning

¤ Severe illness such as meningitis.

¤ Child abuse-- repeated shakings or beatings.

SYMPTOMS

Symptoms may vary considerably depending on the severity and location of brain damage. They may include:

¤ Difficulty in sucking; poor muscle control

¤ Poor coordination

¤ Problems with hearing, seeing , speech

¤ Muscle spasms

¤ Unusual irritability, tenseness

¤ Poor ability to concentrate

¤ Emotional problems

There are several types of cerebral palsy.

¤ SPASTIC-- the most common type is characterized by tense, contracted muscles.

¤ ATHETOID--constant, uncontrolled motion of arms, legs, eyes,head

¤ RIGID--tight muscles that resist efforts to make them move

¤ TREMOR--uncontrollable shaking

¤ ATAXIC--poor sense of balance, causes falls stumbling

These problems may vary from severe to mild, from person to person and from time to time in the same person. Some patients have more than one type of cerebral palsy.

HEARING IMPAIRMENT

Hearing loss can happen before or after birth or it can be inherited. Sometimes the loss is temporary and sometimes it is permanent.

HEARING LOSS HAS MANY CAUSES.

¤ Mother's illness. Certain viral diseases such as rubella can damage cells in the inner ear causing permanent hearing loss in the fetus.

Damage to the ear may occur anytime after birth from:

¤ Accidents--a blow to the head or outer ear may damage the bone chain in the middle ear.

¤ A punctured eardrum from sticking cotton swabs, pencils or other foreign objects into the ear.

¤ Prescription drugs. Certain life-saving drugs may permanently damage hearing.

¤ Fluid in the middle ear (behind the eardrum) caused by colds or allergies. If treated promptly hearing loss may be temporary. If not it may become permanent.

¤ Noises damage hair cells in the inner ear. The noise may be a single sound close to the ear or repeated noise over a long period of time. For example: engine noise such as aircraft, lawn mowers, tractors, loud music or radio, CD or tape player headsets, guns.

¤ Aging. Hearing may be gradually diminished over the years.

¤ Hearing loss may be inherited from mother, father or grandparent.

SHORT GLOSSARY

Hearing impaired: is used to refer to any kind of hearing loss.

Hard of hearing: used to refer to hearing loss which is not as great as 'deaf'.

Deaf: if it is a profound hearing loss.

BLINDNESS

The loss or absence of the ability to see is called blindness. The term, legally blind, applies to any person whose best corrected vision is 20/200 and/or having less than 20 degrees in the visual field. Approximately 1,350,000 persons in the United States are legally blind. About 10% of them are less than twenty years old. More than 50% are over 65 years old. Few people are born blind.

Among the causes of blindness in infants and young children are:

¤ Neglect or unsuitable treatment of inflammation of the eyes of newborn babies.

¤ Malnutrition

¤ Parasitic infections

¤ Infectious diseases

¤ Injuries to the eye or optic nerve, such as cuts, burns, infection, foreign bodies.

¤ Infants of mothers who had rubella (German measles) in early pregnancy also run the risk of impaired vision.

In older persons many become blind through complications from disease or degenerative disorders such as glaucoma, cataracts, or macular degeneration. Diseases such as diabetes and high blood pressure, when not controlled, frequently cause damage to the retina.

HINTS FOR MAKING DISCUSSION MORE EFFECTIVE

The information concerning disabilities is intentionally very brief to provide a simple background for the children. You may wish to contact specific advocacy groups for more in-depth materials for your own information or for working with older young people or adults. See page 84 for a short list.

ABOUT THE DISCUSSION QUESTIONS INCLUDED WITH EACH LESSON

Discussion questions are related to the basic content of the story. The questions are designed to raise awareness about some of the challenges faced by the main characters, as well as highlight similarities they have with children in the class. Finally, students are asked to relate the characters in the story to someone in their class, school, neighborhood or family.

DISCUSSION STARTERS:

As you begin discussion and presentation with the children you may wish to get and keep their interest by using one of the following activities.

¤ Briefly discuss any experiences the children may have had with people having some of the disabilities you will be discussing.

¤ Have the children help make a list of activities that might cause head or spinal cord injuries. They might include falling from a bike or motorcycle when not wearing a helmet, a car accident while not wearing a seat belt, falling from a tree or down the stairs.

EVALUATION:

At the end of every session it is always helpful to evaluate the session while it is fresh in your mind. The following questions may serve as a guideline for evaluating the individual sessions.

¤ In what ways do you feel the session objectives were met?

¤ In what ways did the children show an increased understanding of feelings and frustrations involved in the situations facing the lead character?

¤ Did all the children participate in some way? If they did not, what would you do another time to increase participation?

¤ How did the children show they were involved with the character and the problems of the main characters?

Jot down any ideas that would have made the session more meaningful.

ANDY OPENS WIDE

OBJECTIVE: through story and discussion:

     ¤   to increase awareness and understanding of lifestyle and feelings of those having disabilities.

     ¤   to become aware of the frustrations involved for persons having poor motor control

FOR KINDERGARTEN CHILDREN

Discussion before reading the story:

     ¤ What are some things you can do with your mouth? Show us.

     ¤ Some people can't move their mouths as easily as we can because they were born that way or they might have had their head hurt in a bad accident.

Today we are going to read a story about a little boy who has difficulty doing things with his mouth, but he can do many, many other things just as you and I.

Read: ANDY OPENS WIDE

Discussion:

     ¤ Who is the little boy in this story?

     ¤ Why did Andy have trouble eating his oatmeal?

     ¤ Show me how you open your mouth to eat. That's right, you open wide and then close your mouth and start chewing.

     ¤ Andy had trouble opening his mouth, but he saw all kinds of things that could open wide. What were some things that could open wide?

     ¤ What did Andy do every time he saw something open wide?

     ¤ Do you ever want to hide as Andy did? What do you do when you want to hide?

     ¤ Who took Andy for a ride?

     ¤ Where did he go with his Daddy?

     ¤ What was the surprise Andy had at the feed mill?

     ¤ How do we know Andy liked the puppies?

  ¤ What did he do when his Daddy put him back in the truck?

  ¤ What do you do when you have to stop something you are enjoying?

  ¤ How do we know Andy and his Daddy were happy that he opened wide?

  ¤ What are some things that Andy liked that you like, too?

  ¤ Do you know anyone who has trouble opening his or her mouth as Andy did? Tell us about that person

SUGGESTED ACTIVITIES

Open Wide

    Show me all the ways you can open wide. You can open wide with your mouth, arms, eyes, legs, fingers, toes and even your nose!

Have a Snack

    At snack time have students try to eat without opening their mouths wide. Discuss how they might help a friend like Andy who made a mess when he ate?

FOR ELEMENTARY CHILDREN

    Following a brief presentation of facts concerning disabilities in general and cerebral palsy in particular, the leader may introduce the book with discussion of Andy's problem.

    Andy has a very special problem.

    He can't open his mouth whenever he wants to.

  ¤ What things would be difficult for you to do if you couldn't open your mouth when you wanted to?

  ¤ What things would you need help doing?

Read: ANDY OPENS WIDE

After reading the story you may ask:

  ¤ What problems did Andy have because he couldn't open his mouth when he wanted to?

  ¤ Suppose Andy came to your school and had to eat in your lunchroom. How would his lunch experience be different from yours?

  ¤ What problems do you think Andy would have?

¤ What would be best to do if Andy and his helper were at your table and Andy got food on his face and clothing?

¤ What would be best for Andy to wear when he ate? How do you think the other people at the table would act if the helper put a bib around Andy's neck. What would be the understanding thing to do?

¤ What happened to change Andy's feelings about his problem?

¤ What are some of the things in the story that Andy enjoyed?

¤ List some other things you do that Andy might be able to do and enjoy.

SUGGESTED ACTIVITIES

Role Play (see 'How-to')
Situation:

Choose one person to pretend to be Andy and one person to be Andy's helper. Pretend that you are all seated at the lunch table. Andy is in his wheelchair waiting for his lunch. Decide how you should behave when he has his bib put on and is fed. Act out the lunchroom experience. Discuss things that were good and things that should have been done differently when you have finished.

FOR MIDDLE SCHOOL

Since the book is about a much younger child, the presenter may wish to comment that sometimes it helps to look back on the things we had to attempt as young children to best understand a situation. This story is for and about a young child with cerebral palsy and a problem that was very important to him.

Read: ANDY OPENS WIDE

Discussion:

¤ What was Andy's biggest problem?

¤ What things would be different if you couldn't open your mouth when you wanted to? Let's make a list of the things we do that need oral motor control.

¤ What are some of the things you remember being able to do for yourselves when you were Andy's age? Let's list them.

¤ Which of these things was Andy not able to do for himself?

18

¤ What feelings did Andy show us in this story?

¤ How many of these feelings do we have? Share some examples.

¤ In what ways is Andy different from us or from our brothers and sisters of the same age? In what ways is Andy similar?

SUGGESTED ACTIVITIES

Simulation

Prepare to share a snack time with the class. Have enough cookies on a tray for the entire group. Divide the class into two groups. Tie a scarf around the heads and chins of one group of children. This group is not allowed to move hands or feet. The others move and talk as always. Pass around a tray of cookies. The non-disabled group takes cookies and eats them. They then select a game or book and start another activity. Call time and bring the group together. Untie the group with the disabilities. Ask the tied group how they felt during the snack and play time. Jot down reactions. Ask the non-disabled group for reactions. Encourage discussion of all feelings. When finished, let the other children enjoy a cookie. If time permits you may wish to switch groups and repeat the activity before discussion.

Note: As a follow on story, consider reading and discussing "The Best Face of All", p. 73.

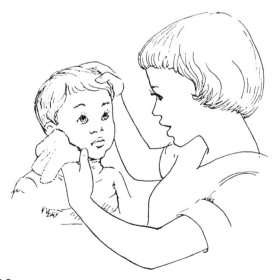

DANNY AND THE MERRY-GO-ROUND

OBJECTIVE: through story and discussion
  ¤ to increase awareness and understanding of lifestyle and feelings of persons with disabilities
  ¤ to help in personal contact between those with disabilities and their nondisabled classmates

FOR KINDERGARTEN CHILDREN

Discussion before reading the story:
  ¤ What are some of the things you can do at a park?
  ¤ What are some of the things that you can do with your legs and feet at the park?

Some people have difficulty moving their legs and feet because their legs or feet don't work just right. They would have difficulty playing as you do. Today we are going to read a story about a little boy who isn't able to walk, but in many ways he is like us.

Read: DANNY AND THE MERRY-GO-ROUND

Discussion:
  ¤ What was the name of the boy in the story?
  ¤ Where did Danny go with his mother?
  ¤ Why didn't Danny like to go to the park?
  ¤ How did it make Danny feel? Have you ever felt left out? Tell me about it.
  ¤ Who was the little girl who came to talk to him?
  ¤ Did she still talk and play with Danny after she found out about his disability?
  ¤ Why did she run off after talking to Danny?
  ¤ Have you ever been on a merry-go-round like the one in the picture? How did you feel at first?
  ¤ How did Danny like the ride?
  ¤ Why was Danny in a wheelchair?
Provide an explanation of his disability. You may wish to re-read Danny's mother's explanation to Liz, directly from the book. Discuss it and correct any misconceptions.
  ¤ Do you know anyone like Danny? Tell us about that person.
  ¤ What would you do if you saw Danny or someone like him in the park?

SUGGESTED ACTIVITIES

Try It Out

If it is possible to have a child's wheelchair available, have the students take turns performing routine activities while in it. Have them get water, wash hands, carry books, etc.. Afterwards, encourage them to talk about the experience.

Let's Pretend

Have one child pretend to be Danny. Someone else may pretend to be Liz. Act out getting acquainted. Take turns as time permits.

FOR ELEMENTARY CHILDREN

Before reading the story present a few facts about disabilities in general and cerebral palsy in particular.
Discussion before reading the story:
¤ How many of you enjoy the playground? Why do you enjoy it?
¤ How would you feel about going to the playground if you had to sit and watch other children play?
You may wish to remind them that even though we know about disabilities, it is sometimes difficult to know how to act when we see a person in a wheelchair or wearing braces for the first time. In the story we are about to read, we meet a little girl who has this experience.

Read: DANNY AND THE MERRY-GO-ROUND.

For Discussion:
¤ In what way was Danny's trip to the playground different from a playtime you might have?
¤ How did Danny feel about going to the playground?
¤ What happened that changed his feelings?
¤ What do you think about the way Liz approached Danny?
¤ What things did Danny learn about himself?
¤ What did Liz learn?

SUGGESTED ACTIVITIES

Make a List

Make a list of activities you think Danny might be able to do with you on the playground. How might you have to change some of them so he could take part in the activity?

Role Play

See the 'How-to' section for directions for conducting a role play situation. If the class has made a list of activities, they may choose to use one. If not, you may wish to discuss possible activities briefly before you begin the role play.

Situation:

Danny is a new boy in your school. You are going to welcome him and invite him to join in your activity. What type of activity will he be able to share with you?

FOR MIDDLE SCHOOL

Since the book is about a much younger child, the presenter may wish to comment that sometimes it helps to look back on the things we had to attempt as young children to best understand a situation. This story is for and about a young child with cerebral palsy and a problem that was very important to him.

Read: DANNY AND THE MERRY-GO-ROUND

Discussion:
¤ What feelings did Danny show in the beginning of the story? when Liz talked to him and his mother? at the end of the story?
¤ What was Danny's problem? How did he feel about himself when he found out what it was?
¤ How did Liz help Danny become more than a spectator on the playground?
¤ Suppose Danny is now eleven years old and is coming to your school for the first time. What are some things that the students can do to make Danny feel happy on the playground?
¤ List ways you can adapt activities or games to include Danny.

SUGGESTED ACTIVITIES

Adapt a Game
Choose a game from the list you have made. Make any changes necessary to make it possible for someone with Danny's abilities to take part with the group. You may wish to take turns playing the part of Danny as you play the game.

Role Play
Using the 'How-to' section and the situation listed in the elementary activity, role play Danny's first day at your school.

Note: For another story about Danny, see "Danny Takes a Special Walk" p.76.

ANDY FINDS A TURTLE

OBJECTIVE: through story and discussion
¤ to increase awareness of persons with disabilities having positive and negative attitudes
¤ to help feel a commonality between those with disabilities and themselves

FOR KINDERGARTEN CHILDREN

Discussion before reading the story:
¤ What are some things you can do with your legs and feet? Encourage the children to talk about or show things they can do with their legs and feet.
¤ What are some things you can do with your arms and hands? Encourage the children to talk about or show things they can do with their arms and hands.
Today we are going to read a story about a little boy who has difficulty walking and moving, but, in many, many ways he is the same as you and I. Let's read about Andy.

Read: ANDY FINDS A TURTLE

Discussion:
¤ What was the boy's name in the story?
¤ Every Monday Andy had physical therapy. He went to physical therapy for exercises that helped make his arms and legs move better. Sometimes he didn't feel like doing his exercises. What did his therapist, Miss Jones, call him when he didn't want to move his legs?
¤ What did his cousin do with Andy in the mornings?
¤ Did Andy know what a turtle was? Do you know what a turtle is?
¤ What did he think a turtle was?
¤ Andy wore a back brace to help hold his spine straight. Where is your spine? Put your fingers on your spine.
¤ What did Andy's cousin call Andy's back brace?
¤ When did Andy find out what a turtle really was?
¤ What are some things that Andy did that we like to do?
¤ Do you know anyone like Andy? Tell us about that person.

SUGGESTED ACTIVITIES
Invite Guests

Invite same age peers who use walkers/wheelchairs to play time with your class. With the help of their teacher plan some activities and games in which everyone can participate.

Invite a Physical Therapist

Have the physical therapist visit your class and do some of Andy's exercises with your students.

FOR ELEMENTARY CHILDREN

Following a brief presentation of facts concerning disabilities in general and cerebral palsy in particular, lead into the story by talking about how we sometimes don't feel like being helpful. We just don't want to try to help our parents, our teachers or even do things for ourselves.

Discussion before the story:

¤ Do you always feel like getting out of bed in the morning? How many like to go to bed at night?

¤ How many of you have something that you have to do, at school or at home, that you dislike doing? How do you show that you don't feel like being helpful?

Today we're going to hear a story about Andy. He has cerebral palsy so in some ways he is quite different from each of you but in some ways he is very much like you. He doesn't always like to be helpful, especially when it's time to do his exercises with his physical therapist, or PT, as she is called in the story.

Read: ANDY FINDS A TURTLE

Discussion:

¤ Why didn't Andy want to cooperate with his PT?

¤ Why was it important for him to exercise with the PT?

¤ What are some things we have to do that are helpful to us that we don't always feel like doing?

¤ Why don't we want to cooperate with some of these actions?

¤ If we don't understand something, what do we do? Why didn't Andy ask about a turtle?

¤ How does the ending make you feel about Andy?

"Danny and The Ivy", p.75, would be a fun story to read as a follow-on story.

SUGGESTED ACTIVITY
    Think of or write down one thing that you do not feel like doing. Think of why it is as important for you to do that thing as it was for Andy to do PT. Write a story about it or draw a picture that tells about it.

FOR MIDDLE SCHOOL

    After presenting brief facts about disabilities in general, the presenter may wish to introduce the session in this way:
    This book is about a child who is much younger than any of you. It often helps to look back on attitudes and feelings that we had as young children to understand how we think and feel today. This story is about a young child with cerebral palsy who wasn't able to ask about things being done to and for him and therefore didn't want to be helpful.

Read: ANDY FINDS A TURTLE.

Discussion:
    ¤ Do any of you remember having to do certain things and you couldn't understand why they had to be done?
    ¤ Do you remember any experience that was frightening or confusing that no one explained, possibly an x-ray or a visit to the hospital that might have been confusing or scary?
    ¤ Describe Andy's feelings at the beginning of the story, then at the end of the story.
    ¤ What could have been done to make Andy feel more cooperative?

SUGGESTED ACTIVITIES

Finding Your Turtle
    Make a list of things you don't really like to do or that make you feel uncooperative. Beside each item write the reason it is important to do. If you don't understand why it is important, decide how you will find out about it. Who will you ask?

Help Someone Else Find Their Turtle
    If you have a younger brother or sister, think about what makes them have a temper, or become frightened or uncooperative.   Think about what you can do to help them understand why they must cooperate. Draw a picture to share with them and to discuss their fears or frustrations.

PATRICK AND EMMA LOU

OBJECTIVE: through story and discussion
      ¤ to increase awareness of similarities between children with disabilities and non-disabled children
      ¤ to explore contrast between inside feelings and actual accomplishment

FOR KINDERGARTEN CHILDREN

Discussion before reading the story:
      ¤ What are some things you can do with your legs and feet?

Walking is hard for some people for different reasons. Some people have difficulty walking because they have been in an accident. For others the problem may have started when they were born. Today we're going to read a story about two children who have difficulty walking, but they can do many, many other things that we do.

Read: PATRICK AND EMMA LOU

Discussion:
      ¤ Who were the children in this story?
      ¤ What did Emma Lou do when she first saw Patrick?
      ¤ Why did she do that?
      ¤ What were Patrick and Emma Lou learning to do?
      ¤ What are they using to help them walk?
      ¤ Why do they wear braces on their legs?
      ¤ Was it easy for Patrick to walk with his walker?
      ¤ What happened when he did not pay attention?
        Who was cheering him on?
      ¤ What is something you are learning how to do that is hard for you?
        Who cheers you on?
      ¤ How do you feel when someone cheers you on? Who do you cheer on?
      ¤ What are some things Patrick and Emma Lou can do that we can do?
      ¤ Do you know anyone like Patrick and Emma Lou? Tell us about them.

SUGGESTED ACTIVITIES
Try a Walker

Have a walker and braces available for children to explore. Encourage children to move with the walker around the room. Allow children to try on the braces. Discuss how these pieces of equipment are *not* toys, but equipment that helps people move around more easily.

A Relay

Have a relay with feet loosely tied together to simulate difficulty with walking and balance. After relay encourage children to talk about the experience.

FOR ELEMENTARY CHILDREN

Begin the session with a discussion of physical disabilities in general and specifics about spina bifida and cerebral palsy.

Discussion before reading the story:

¤ How many of you remember when you learned to walk ? Comment that not many remember. Learning to walk for most of the children happened before or soon after they were a year old.

¤ How many have younger brothers or sisters, neighbors who are just beginning to walk? Encourage discussion of the problems involved.

You may wish to introduce the story further by discussing briefly disabilities that may make walking difficult or you may choose to read the story followed by discussion.

Read: PATRICK AND EMMA LOU.

Discussion:

¤ What was so special about that Monday morning for Patrick?

¤ What did Patrick and Emma Lou have on their legs? Why did they wear braces?

¤ What did Patrick use to get around? What did Emma Lou use?

¤ Was it easy for Patrick to walk with the walker? What problems did he have? What happened when he forgot to look up and steer?

¤ Why do you think Emma Lou stuck out her tongue at Patrick?

Allow opportunity to discuss how uncomfortable it is to be stared at. You may wish to explore the reasons behind staring at others.

SUGGESTED ACTIVITIES

Look around your room. What would you have to change or rearrange so Patrick and Emma Lou could move around easily with a walker or wheelchair? Decide what you could do to help them get around in your room. What kind of help might make them feel uncomfortable?

FOR MIDDLE SCHOOL

After presenting disability facts, answer any questions that may come up concerning disabilities.

The presenter may then wish to introduce the session in this way:

This book is about a child who is much younger than any of you. Many of you may have younger brothers, sisters or friends who have been learning to walk and will understand some of the problems they may have had. Patrick's desire to walk was the same but his problems were greater.

Read: PATRICK AND EMMA LOU

Discussion:

You may wish to ask selected questions from those listed for use in elementary classes in addition to some of the following:

¤ How did Patrick feel about walking when he first arrived? after he had tried to use the walker? after he and Emma Lou went for a walk in the hall?

¤ What have you tried to do--imagined yourself doing-- only to discover when you tried to do it, it wasn't easy? Discuss any feelings the students had when they first tried and after they had worked hard to learn it.

¤ Patrick and Emma Lou can't walk, run or jump as well as most of the children in the class, but they are able to do and enjoy some things as well as you can. Make a list of things they may be able to do.

SUGGESTED ACTIVITIES

Plan a Party

Plan a class party for the next holiday that would include activities everyone, including Patrick and Emma Lou, could enjoy. Invite a special education class to the party.

Make a List

Make a list of things that are worth doing that take a lot of practice and concentration. Choose one that you will work very hard learning just as Patrick and Emma Lou were doing when they were learning to walk.

SMILE FROM ANDY

OBJECTIVE: through story and discussion to
¤ highlight similarities in feelings/activities
¤ become aware of the importance of personal contact between children with disabilities and those who are non-disabled.

FOR KINDERGARTEN CHILDREN

Discussion before reading the story:
¤ What are some things you can do with your legs and feet? Encourage children to talk about or show things they can do with their legs and feet.

Some people have difficulty moving their legs and feet because their legs or feet don't work just right. Today we are going to read a story about a little boy who is shy and can't walk. He can do many, many things that you and I can do. Let's read about Andy.

Read: A SMILE FROM ANDY

Discussion:
¤ How did Andy feel when he met people? Why do you think he felt like that?
¤ Do you ever feel shy like Andy? When do you feel shy?
¤ What did he do when people talked to his baby sister? Andy's sister got a lot of attention at the mall. How do you feel when your brother or sister or friend gets all the attention?
¤ What did Andy see in the mall?
¤ Do you like to go to the mall like Andy? What do you do at the mall?
¤ Why didn't Andy like sitting in his chair?
¤ What happened when Liz talked to him?
¤ Why does Andy use a wheelchair?
¤ Do you know anyone like Andy? Tell us about that person.
¤ If you saw a child like Andy in the mall, what could you do?

If asked, provide explanation of a person who is in a wheelchair and correct any misconceptions that are given. You may wish to explain that sometimes a person has trouble walking because they were in an accident or sometimes because they were born that way.

SUGGESTED ACTIVITIES
Plan a Trip
Plan a trip to the mall with same age peers who use walkers and wheelchairs. Plan the trip, working closely with their teacher.

Draw a Picture
Have students draw a picture of Andy at the mall.
Ask the students to put themselves in the picture, showing what they would do if they saw Andy at the mall.

FOR ELEMENTARY CHILDREN

Following a brief presentation or review of facts concerning cerebral palsy, lead into the story by talking briefly about feeling shy or left out.
¤ How many of you have ever felt shy? Share experiences about feeling shy or left out.
¤ How do you feel when a brother or sister or classmate gets all the attention and you are ignored?
Today we are going to hear a story about Andy. Andy has cerebral palsy. He can't walk or talk, but he wants people to notice him .

Read : A SMILE FROM ANDY.

Discussion:
¤ What did Andy want people to do when they saw him?
¤ How did he feel when they talked to his baby sister? What did he do?
¤ What are some things that make you feel grim like Andy?
¤ What did he want to do instead of sitting in his chair?
¤ What happened when Liz came and talked to him? How did everyone feel then?
¤ Think of a time when you have felt grim. Did something make you smile? How did you feel then?

SUGGESTED ACTIVITY

Role Play (see the 'How-to' section for suggestions)
Situation:
Pretend that you are at the mall and see another person who is in a wheelchair, who is looking unhappy or left out. Act out how you could make that person feel less left out as Liz did with Andy.

Make a Mural

See the 'How-to' section for specific directions.

Make a mural of the things that Andy enjoyed at the mall that you also enjoy. Make additions of things that you have at your mall that Andy didn't have but would enjoy.

FOR MIDDLE SCHOOL

Present facts or review facts about disabilities in general as well as specific information about cerebral palsy. Discuss any questions or experiences the children may wish to share.

Before reading the story discuss experiences the children may have had when they have felt shy or embarrassed. Talk about experiences they have had when others have received attention and they have wished they could. You may remind them that, though Andy is much younger than some of them, his feelings and reactions to people around him are the same as many of their feelings and reactions.

Read: A SMILE FROM ANDY.

Discussion:

¤ Why was Andy in a wheel chair? If this is the first time the children have met Andy, take time to present some facts and discuss cerebral palsy
¤ How did Andy feel when he met people? Why did he feel this way?
¤ What would Andy have liked to be doing?
¤ Who finally came and talked to him?
¤ What did he discover about himself?
¤ Did you ever feel like Andy? How do you feel when a brother or sister or friend gets a lot of attention?
¤ How helpful do you think a big smile would be if you were feeling shy and grim? Why?

SUGGESTED ACTIVITIES

Write a Poem

In a way Andy felt invisible until Liz paid attention to him. Write a poem about Andy's feelings as an invisible person and then the joy of being noticed.

Make a Montage

For specific directions see the 'How-to' section.

Have the children decide what the subject of the montage will be. They may wish to show:

- the excitement and happiness of the mall.
- feelings of shyness and then acceptance
- things that they have in common with Andy.

Note: For a story about a special friendship read and discuss "The Champions" by Nan Holcomb, p. 80.

FAIR AND SQUARE

OBJECTIVE: through story and discussion
> ¤ to increase understanding of fairness in playing with people with disabilities
> ¤ to increase understanding feelings shared in winning or losing experiences

FOR KINDERGARTEN CHILDREN

Discussion before reading the story:
> ¤ What are some things you can do with your arms and hands? Encourage children to talk about or show things they can do with their arms and hands.
> Today we are going to read a story about a little boy named Kevin, who can't use his hands, but, he can enjoy many, many other things that we enjoy.

Read: FAIR AND SQUARE

Discussion:
> ¤ Who was the little boy in the story?
> ¤ Who was Jill? Don?
> ¤ What kinds of games did they play at home?
> ¤ Why did Kevin start crying , even though he won the game?
> ¤ Have you ever felt like Kevin? Tell us about it.
> ¤ What did Miss Wells have for Kevin at school?
> ¤ What happened when Kevin first started using the control switch to move the car?
> ¤ Who went to school for play day?
> ¤ When they played computer rocket, who won the most?
> ¤ Why wasn't Kevin sad when he lost?
> ¤ What are some games that you can win, fair and square, without any help?
> ¤ Do you know anyone like Kevin? Tell me about that person.
> ¤ What could you do if you had a friend like Kevin who had trouble playing a game?

SUGGESTED ACTIVITIES

Take a Trip
> Plan to visit a class of same age peers with disabilities for some games. Together with their teacher, determine the kinds of games and activities in which everyone can take part.

Use a Switch

Contact a therapist to bring in a switch to use with a computer, or go to the therapy department and try using a switch to guide a remote control car, or play a game. Have children take turns.

FOR ELEMENTARY CHILDREN

You may begin with a few general facts about disabilities and some of the particular problems involved in having extremely limited use of hands.
Before reading the story you may wish to ask:
¤ Have any of you ever played a game with an older person who 'let' you win? How did you feel?
¤ Have you ever wanted to play with a toy and were told that you were too little or unable to do it? What did you do?

Read: FAIR AND SQUARE.

Discussion:
¤ What things did Kevin want to do before someone finally got around to playing with him?
¤ What do you think of the way Don and Jill played with him?
¤ What did Kevin think about the way they played with him?
¤ How could Don and Jill have made game playing a happy experience for Kevin?
¤ What did Kevin learn to do in therapy?
¤ What was the thing called that Kevin used to play on the computer?
¤ How did the switch help Kevin play fair and square?
¤ What other things could Kevin play using the computer switch?
¤ What happened when his family visited school and played a game with him?
¤ Kevin said that Don could learn to win. "all it takes is work!" Name some things you like to play that you need to work at to learn to do well.

SUGGESTED ACTIVITY

Simulation: (See 'How-to section)
Choose a game that your class enjoys. Have half of the group pretend they are Brian or Kevin. The rest of the class will be Don or Jill. First, have Dons and Jills play the game as they always do while the Brians and Kevins watch.

35

¤ How did the Dons and Jills feel?

¤ How did the Brians and Kevins feel?

Discuss how it could have been a more enjoyable experience for both groups. If time permits try it again following the suggestions.

FOR MIDDLE SCHOOL

Before reading the story discuss experiences the children may have had playing games with younger children or recall times when they were much younger and someone may have let them win.

Discuss feelings, talk about reasons for 'letting' people win a game.

Read: FAIR AND SQUARE.

Discussion:

¤ How did Kevin feel when others were playing and he was put off with promises? Why do you think people do this?

¤ What did Kevin think about the way Don and Jill played with him?

¤ Why do you think they cheated for him?

¤ What is a switch?

¤ What was so great about it for Kevin and Brian?

¤ Kevin said that Don could learn to win. "All it takes is work!" Name some things that you like to play that you need to work at to learn to do well.

SUGGESTED ACTIVITY

Plan a Game

Choose two or three favorite games you all enjoy playing. Decide how these can be played with two people from your group and two people from a group of children having limited use of their hands. Plan to invite a group for a game playing party.

Best and Worst

Have each person jot down a game or sport that they do best and one that they do worst. Make a list of BEST on the board and one marked WORST. Decide which are worst because the person lacks ability or just needs instruction and practice. Pretend you are planning a party for the class. Which activities would you use so everyone could have a good time?

HOW ABOUT A HUG

OBJECTIVE: through reading and discussion to
- ¤ become aware of the effort it takes for some people with Down syndrome to accomplish things we take for granted
- ¤ realize how important it is to share happy moments with friends and family

FOR KINDERGARTEN CHILDREN

Discussion before reading the story:
- ¤ Name some things that are easy for you to do. Name some things that are hard for you to do. All of us are good at doing some things and have difficulty doing other things.
- ¤ What does your mommy, daddy, or teacher do to help you when you are having trouble doing something?

Today we are going to read a story about a little girl, who, like us, does some things that are easy for her and some things that are difficult for her.

Read: HOW ABOUT A HUG

Discussion:
- ¤ Who wakes the little girl up in the morning? What does her mommy give her? That's right! Give yourself a hug!
- ¤ What does she do with Daddy's help? That's right! Give yourself a hug!
- ¤ What does she do with Grandma's help? Who gives her a hug? That's right! Give yourself a hug!
- ¤ Who hugs you at home? Show me how you hug your brother or sister.
- ¤ When the little girl gets to school, who does she see?
- ¤ What did she do with her school grandmother?
- ¤ The story tells us that she buttoned a vest and put on her shoes. Can you put your shoes on? Show me. Can you tie your shoes? Show me.
- ¤ Ask a friend, "How about a hug?" If your friend says 'yes', give that friend a hug! What do you do if your friend says, "no"?

Encourage children to talk about times when they do not want a hug. It is OK to say, "No."
- ¤ Do you know anyone like the little girl in the story? Tell us about that person.

SUGGESTED ACTIVITIES

Invite Guests
     Invite same age peers who have developmental delays to play time with your class. Plan activities and games with their teacher in which everyone can participate.

Draw a Picture
     Some things are easy for us, and some things are hard for us. Just like it was for the little girl, it is sometimes easier to do things when someone gives us a hug.
     Think of something that is difficult for you to do. Draw a picture of yourself doing it. Give yourself a hug for it because you have done it right.

FOR ELEMENTARY SCHOOL

     Using materials from the introduction, presents facts in general about disabilities followed by specifics of Down Syndrome.
     Before reading the story you may wish to discuss differences in accomplishing skills among people who are non-disabled. You may talk about when each child learned to tie shoes, skip or write their names in cursive. Some other tasks that take shorter, or longer times depending on individual interest and development might be making a bed or learning number facts.
     You may introduce the story by saying, "In our story the little girl has Down syndrome. She can learn but, just as each of us do some things easily and some things slower than others in the class, she has to learn at her own speed."

Read: HOW ABOUT A HUG.

Discussion:
     ¤ Who were some of the helpers in the story? What were some of the things they helped her do?
     ¤ Why do you think she had to have help walking the balance beam? (to help develop her large muscles that will help make her walk straight and steady)
     ¤ What things did she do that you enjoy doing?
     ¤ What things do you think you would do for fun if she spent the afternoon with you?
     ¤ What do you think about the 'hugs'? How does it help to have people happy with you when you're trying to learn a new task?

SUGGESTED ACTIVITY

Draw a Picture
   Draw a picture of something you have trouble doing that you need some cheers and hugs to help make you try harder.

FOR MIDDLE SCHOOL

   Present the facts about Down syndrome from sensitivity and awareness introduction material. Discuss any experiences they may have had with persons with Down syndrome or, who may not physically disabled, but may have learning problems. Introduce the story by telling them that the story was written for and about a much younger child but as they listen they may try to think about some things they learned that were not easy for them to learn. Think about times when someone helped them and shared their happiness when they did the thing correctly.

Read: HOW ABOUT A HUG.

Discussion:
   ¤ What things do you notice that are different about this child from other children her age.
   ¤ What things are the same?
   ¤ What things did she enjoy that you enjoyed doing when you were six years old?
   ¤ Suppose she came to your school now. How do you think she would be different from the rest of you in your class?
   ¤ What things might she have difficulty doing?
   ¤ What help might she expect from you?
   ¤ How would you act when she tried and tried and finally succeeded?
   ¤ What attitudes would be harmful and might keep her from learning? What might help her develop and be happy?

SUGGESTED ACTIVITY
Make a List
   Pretend you have friends or classmates who have learning disabilities or possibly Down syndrome. Make a list of things you do that would make them happy and help them succeed.
   Make a list of things you would *not* do or say as it would make them unhappy and insecure.

COOKIE

OBJECTIVE: through story and discussion
> ¤ to become aware of signing as a way of opening communication channels with children who have limited verbal skills
> ¤ to open areas of understanding between non-disabled children and those who have disabilities

FOR KINDERGARTEN CHILDREN

Discussion before reading the story:
> Some people have difficulty talking. Sometimes, they learn a new way to say things by using their hands. I believe you know how to say some things with your hands! Show me how you say goodbye using your hands. Show me what you want using your hands, not your voice. Show me how you say 'yes' and 'no' without speaking. You know lots of ways to tell me things!
> Today we are going to read a story about a little girl named Molly. Molly has Down syndrome and so has difficulty talking, but, she can do many, many other things that we do. Let's read about Molly.

Read: COOKIE

Discussion:
> ¤ Who was the little girl in the story?
> ¤ What are some things Molly made with blocks?
> ¤ When Molly got hungry what did she want? Some cheese? Some lettuce? Some milk?
> ¤ How did she try to reach the cookie?
> ¤ Why was her mommy upset when she saw Molly on the chair?
> ¤ How did Molly feel when her mother didn't understand her? Do you ever feel like Molly?
> ¤ Who came to help Molly?
> ¤ How did Susan help Molly learn to tell her mommy what she wanted?
> ¤ Even though Molly could not talk, she could do lots of things you enjoy doing. Who likes to build things with blocks like Molly? What do you like to build?
> ¤ Molly helped her mommy set the table. Do you help set the table at your house? What do you put on the table?
> ¤ Do you play with anyone like Molly? How could you talk to that person?

SUGGESTED ACTIVITIES
Have a Snack

What two words did Susan teach Molly to say with her hands? Can you show me the sign for cookie? for juice? Have a snack of juice and cookies. Practice the signs for cookie, juice.

Learn a Sign

Have a sign language chart available. Select a few simple words such as 'hello', 'love', 'lunch' for children to practice using sign language with you.

FOR ELEMENTARY CHILDREN

Following a brief presentation of facts concerning disabilities in general and Down syndrome in particular, introduce the book, COOKIE.
Discussion before reading the story:
¤ Have any of you ever wanted something but the person you were trying to talk to didn't understand and gave you something else?
¤ Do any of you have younger brothers or sisters who can't talk very well? Think of a time to share when your brother or sister cried or became angry because you didn't understand what was wanted.
The story today is about a little girl named Molly who couldn't talk well enough to ask for the things she wanted-- until a special person taught her a new way to talk.

Read: COOKIE.

Discussion:
¤ What did Molly want after she finished playing with the blocks?
¤ Where did she look for something to eat?
¤ When she didn't find what she wanted, what did she do?
¤ What did her mother say about her climbing on the chair?
¤ Did her mother suggest anything Molly wanted?
¤ So then what did Molly do?
¤ Who came to help Molly with her problem?
¤ What did the speech therapist do to help Molly?
¤ What did Molly do that you like to do?
¤ Do you ever get angry when people don't understand what you want? Share a time when this has happened to you.
¤ What other things did Molly do that you often do?

Note:
The children might enjoy listening to: "The Best Cookie Eater in Town" p74.

SUGGESTED ACTIVITIES
Learn a sign
Learn to sign "cookie" and "juice". Have a snack of cookies and juice.

FOR MIDDLE SCHOOL

Discuss facts about disabilities. Discuss Down syndrome in more detail using the notes in the opening chapter.

Before reading the story discuss experiences the children may have had with problems of communication either being understood or understanding others. You may remind them that, though Molly is very young, there are many people of all ages who are not able to talk. They all have feelings of frustration as do those who are trying to communicate with them.

Read: COOKIE.

After reading the story:
¤ Encourage the children to share experiences and to ask questions about Molly's frustration.
¤ Explore other conditions besides Down syndrome that they may have come in contact with that interfere with communication.
¤ Discuss things they can do to help in understanding and communication in these instances.

SUGGESTED ACTIVITIES
Learn to use Signs
You may use the dictionary of signs included in the Turtle Book, WHEN I GROW UP, or locate and bring in books or videos of signing from your school or public library for this activity. Using these, have the class prepare a simple conversation.

Keep it very simple if this is a first experience.

Simulation:
Plan a party
Divide the group into two sections. One group is unable to talk. The other group answers all questions verbally. Write suggestions on the board. Prepare simple questions, such as: What games shall we play? What shall we eat? Who shall we invite? What committees shall we have? You may try to include the non-verbal, but don't take too long trying to understand. Go quickly to someone who is speaking. End the simulation and discuss how they felt about the experience.

SARAH'S SURPRISE

OBJECTIVE: through story and discussion
    ¤ to highlight similarities between children with disabilities and children without disabilities
    ¤ to explore some ways people communicate with each other

FOR KINDERGARTEN CHILDREN

Discussion before reading the story:

    Some people have difficulty talking as you and I talk. Sometimes, they learn a new way to say things by using their hands. I believe you know how to say some things with your hands! Show me how you say goodbye using your hands. Show me something that you want using your hands, not your voice. Show me how you say 'yes' and 'no' without speaking. You know lots of ways to tell me things!

    Some people also use pictures to show what they want. Today we are going to read a story about a little girl named Sarah. Sarah cannot talk with words, but she talks using a Touch Talker. Let's read about Sarah and find out about her special way of talking.

Read: SARAH'S SURPRISE

Discussion:
    ¤ Who was the little girl in the story?
    ¤ Whose birthday was she getting ready for? Why was Sarah sad?
    ¤ Why wouldn't Sarah watch the cartoons with Jay and Julie?
    ¤ How did Jay try to cheer her up?
    ¤ Do you ever make cards for your mothers? What do you draw?
    ¤ What does Sarah do with her peas at dinner? Why does she do this? Do you ever do things like that?
    ¤ How do you feel when you are trying to tell someone something and that person does not understand you? What do you do when you get frustrated?
    ¤ If you could not talk, how would you tell me what you wanted?
    ¤ How did Sarah talk? How did Sarah sing for her mom?
    ¤ Do you know anyone like Sarah? How do you think you might talk with that person?

Children like Sarah cannot talk as we do but they can talk to us in different ways. If you were unable to talk as you do, you could use your hands, talking with sign language. You could point to pictures, or you could use a computer. Sarah talks using a computer and pointing to pictures to tell what she wants to say. Her computer was called a Touch Talker.

SUGGESTED ACTIVITIES
Use a Communication Board
Have a communication board available for children to explore. Encourage children to communicate using it. Discuss how this equipment is *not* a toy, but, equipment that helps people communicate more easily.

Make a Picture Board
Have children make a communication board as a class. Discuss the pictures and words they will need to put on it to let people know their daily needs. Follow the directions included for elementary children.

FOR ELEMENTARY CHILDREN

Following a brief presentation of facts about disabilities, you may wish to focus on some of the disabilities that contribute to communication disorders.

Before reading the story you may wish to discuss ways they have observed people communicating without talking. You may stimulate this discussion by saying:

"I would like to have each one of you think of something you would like to tell me. Then think of some way to communicate it to me without using words."

Give them a few moments then choose three or four to communicate their message to you without speaking. When the children seem to be involved, you may explain that Sarah has cerebral palsy and it has affected her ability to speak. Sarah talks using a picture board and a computer. Sarah wants to do more than talk. The story, SARAH'S SURPRISE, tells you about her special wish.

Read: SARAH'S SURPRISE.

Discussion:
    ¤ What did Sarah want to do to help celebrate her Mom's birthday?
    ¤ How did she do it?
    ¤ How many other ways did they say 'Happy Birthday'?
    ¤ What celebration things did Sarah do that you like to do?
    ¤ Have any of you ever given food you didn't like to the dog when no one was looking?
    ¤ How did Sarah feel when Jay and Julie didn't understand what she wanted?
    ¤ How do you feel when you try to tell someone something and they don't understand?

SUGGESTED ACTIVITY

Make a Picture Board.

Study the picture on page 18 in SARAH'S SURPRISE. Decide what words and ideas you want to include in your picture board. You will need a large sheet of poster board or construction paper. Draw lines vertically and horizontally to make squares about 1 1/2". Draw the pictures or cut out and paste small pictures from magazines to express your ideas. You may wish to use both drawings and cut outs. When it is finished, use it to tell a friend about your birthday, vacation or your family.

FOR MIDDLE SCHOOL

Present general background material about disabilities. Discuss specific disabilities that may contribute to communication problems.   Answer any questions they may have at this time.

Before reading the story you may wish to discuss ways they have observed people communicating without talking. You might signal a few directions to them without words, such as:

SHUT THE DOOR—point to a child. Motion to shut or open a door or window.
STAND UP— indicate with hand motion followed by SIT DOWN.
HUSH OR QUIET—finger to the lips, etc.

When the children seem to be involved, you may discuss the difficulties in depending on that sort of communication. You may explain that Sarah, the girl in our story today, has cerebral palsy and it has affected her ability to speak. Sarah talks using a picture board and a computer, but Sarah wants to do more than talk. The story, SARAH'S SURPRISE, tells you about her special wish.

Read: SARAH'S SURPRISE.

Discussion:
    ¤ What did Sarah want to do to help celebrate her mother's birthday?
    ¤ How did she do it?
    ¤ What celebration things did Sarah do that you like to do?
    ¤ How do you think Sarah felt when Jay and Julie didn't understand her?
    ¤ How do you feel when you try to tell someone something and they don't understand?
    ¤ Julie and Jay were playing a game similar to a game of charades when they were trying to communicate with Sarah (p.12) in the story. Let's play a game of charades and see how well we can communicate with each other.

CHARADES

Divide the group into two teams, one of guessers and one team of players. Give the team of players prepared slips of paper having words to be pantomimed for the team of guessers.

Have a person on the player side hold up fingers to tell the guessers the number of syllables the word has. Then hold up one finger to show that they will act out the first syllable. Do the same for the second and third syllables.
Some words might be sandwich, playful, candlestick, neighborhood.

One or two players, as needed, will act out each syllable for the guessers to either guess or give up. When the game has continued for one or two words, stop the play and discuss what has happened.

¤ What do you think about this as a way of letting people know what you want or need?

¤ What other ways did Sarah use to communicate? Read pages 12 and 17 again if needed.

¤ Why was the computer so special for Sarah?

SUGGESTED ACTIVITIES

You may wish to continue the game of Charades or make a picture board and communicate an idea using it.

NOTES

BUDDY'S SHADOW

OBJECTIVE: through story and discussion
- ¤ to become aware that everyone needs friends, those who have disabilities and those who do not
- ¤ to explore ways children who have varying skills may be included in play activities

FOR KINDERGARTEN CHILDREN

Discussion before reading the story:
- ¤ Name some things that are easy for you to do.
- ¤ Name some things that are hard for you to do. All of us are good at doing some things and have difficulty doing other things.

Today we are going to read a story about a little boy named Buddy. Buddy has Down syndrome. Some things are easy for him and some things are hard for him, just as they are for us.

Read: BUDDY'S SHADOW

Discussion:
- ¤ Who was the little boy in the story?
- ¤ What were some of the things the children were playing on the playground?
- ¤ What are some fun things you can do on the playground?
- ¤ What things are easy for you to do on the playground? What things are hard for you to do?
- ¤ How did Buddy feel when he could not catch the ball or run as fast as his friends? Do you ever feel like Buddy ? Tell us about it.
- ¤ What was Buddy's secret?
- ¤ Have you ever saved money for something special? What did you buy with your money?
- ¤ Who could run faster, the boys or the dog?
- ¤ How did the puppy scare Buddy?
- ¤ Where did the puppy sleep that night? Have you ever slept with a puppy?
- ¤ Why was Buddy glad to have a puppy?
- ¤ Do you know someone like Buddy? Tell us about that person.
- ¤ Pretend Buddy is coming to our class. Since he can't run as fast or catch a ball as well as the rest of us, what could we do to make him feel that he belongs?

SUGGESTED ACTIVITIES:
Shadow Play

Darken the room. Using a spotlight or flashlight, allow children to take turns making shadows on the wall.

If it is a sunny day, play a game of shadow chase outside. If you step on the person's shadow, they are caught.

Make a Picture

Make a picture about the story using an assortment of materials such as furry cloth, crayons, newsprint.

FOR ELEMENTARY SCHOOL

Present facts about disabilities in general with more specific information about Down syndrome. Answer any questions as they arise.

Before reading the story you may discuss differences we all have in skills. Some may run very fast. Some may catch or throw balls better than others. Some may read better or do math better. Ask if these differences keep others from being our friends. Why or why not?

Tell the children to listen to the story and try to discover what Buddy thought about these differences.

Read: BUDDY'S SHADOW.

Discussion:
¤ What was Buddy's secret?
¤ Have any of you ever saved and saved to buy something special? Share experiences in saving and projects saved for.
¤ How did the puppy get its name?
¤ Why did Buddy want a puppy?
¤ What things did Buddy enjoy doing that you also like to do?
¤ How many of you have a best friend? Why do you like your best friend? Why did you choose that person?
¤ Have you ever *not* had a best friend but wanted one?

SUGGESTED ACTIVITIES
Make a List

Pretend Buddy will be on the playground today during recess. List some things you can play so Buddy won't feel left out. Discuss ways to play your favorite games so Buddy will enjoy them. Add them to your list.

Draw a Picture

Draw a picture of something you would like to do with Buddy that would make him feel good about being your friend.

FOR MIDDLE SCHOOL

Introduce general information concerning physical disabilities and more specific information about Down syndrome.

Introduce the story using some of the ideas for the elementary classes. Emphasize the differences we all share in attaining special skills in sports, art, music, math or reading.

Read: BUDDY'S SHADOW.

Discussion:

¤ Have any of you ever moved to a new school and didn't have any friends for a while? Share feelings about this experience.

¤ Why are friends important?

¤ What kind of people need to have friends? Do grownups need friends? Do teen agers? Do children? How about people who look different or have disabilities?

¤ How many of you have a best friend? Why do you have a best friend?

¤ Why did you choose this person as your best friend?

¤ Think of a way you might help someone like Buddy feel a sense of belonging and friendship in your class.

SUGGESTED ACTIVITY

Plan an activity to share with a group of children who have disabilities similar to Buddy's. Keep in mind that they may be able to do the same things your class does, but they will do them more slowly. You may wish to work in pairs, walk instead of run to play a game, pass a ball instead of throwing it or throw shorter distances than you would ordinarily throw.

Make a list of favorite relay races. Choose some that can be adapted for people with skills like Buddy has. Plan to use some of them for a field day you will share with a special education group.

Note: "Peer Buddies: I Can Help" by Judy Foil p.78, would be a good follow-on for further discussion.

49

WHEN I GROW UP

OBJECTIVE: through story and discussion
¤ to increase awareness and importance of signing as an alternative communication for persons with hearing impairment.
¤ to become aware of the fact that hearing impairment has many causes and can occur at any time of life.
¤ to become aware of similarities they all may share in wondering about "When I grow up..."

FOR KINDERGARTEN CHILDREN

Discussion before reading the story:
¤ What are some of the things you can hear right now?
¤ Some people have difficulty hearing because their ears do not work just right. Today we are going to read a story about a little boy who is deaf, but, who can do many, many other things that we can do. Let's read about Jimmy.

Read: WHEN I GROW UP

Discussion:
¤ Who was the little boy in the story?
¤ How did he talk to his mother? Why did he talk using sign language?
¤ Let's see if we can learn to sign some words. Who remembers how Jimmy said, 'Mom'?
¤ What was the first stop they made on the bus trip?
¤ How did the zoo smell? Show me the sign for 'stink'.
¤ What happened to Jimmy at the elephant park?
¤ Let's all try the sign for 'elephant'.
¤ Tell me about the woman who took care of the elephants.
¤ Where did they go next?
¤ What did Patty make?
¤ Patty said that she was deaf. What does it mean to be deaf?
¤ What other people did they visit?
¤ How did all these other people talk to the children?
¤ What is a hearing aid? (You may wish to explain that it is like a tiny loud speaker or amplifier that fits in the ear, and helps a person hear better. Some people wear one hearing aid. Some people wear two.)
¤ Do you know anyone who wears a hearing aid? Tell us about that person.

SUGGESTED ACTIVITIES
Use Signs

       Have a conversation using as many signs as possible from the story.

Invite Guests

       Invite same age peers who use sign language to play time with your class. Together with their teacher, determine activities/games in which everyone could participate.

Draw a Picture

       Ask, "What do you want to do when you grow up?" Talk about the things necessary to do it. Must they be able to hear? walk? talk? see? to do that thing?

       Have them draw a picture of themselves doing what they would like to do when they grow up.

FOR ELEMENTARY SCHOOL

       Discuss disabilities in general and conditions causing hearing impairment. Answer any questions or share experiences they may have had with relatives or friends of the family who may have hearing impairment. Talk about some of the causes of hearing loss that can happen all through life.

Read: WHEN I GROW UP.

Discussion:

       ¤ How did Jimmy 'talk' with his mother?

       ¤ What did he ask about hearing and speaking when he grew up?

       ¤ What was the big question he had about growing up?

       ¤ How many of you ever wonder what you'll be when you grow up? Share ideas briefly.

       ¤ Recall some of the experiences the children had on the bus trip, discussing ways the people communicated. Discuss how other talents were more important to the job than hearing was.

SUGGESTED ACTIVITIES
Learn Some Signs.

       Assign a word to sign to each child. Give any help needed to help them learn the sign. Re-read the story having the children sign at their individual word in the story.

Draw a Picture

Have the children draw pictures showing what they would like to be when they grow up. Discuss talents they have that would make this special for them.

FOR MIDDLE SCHOOL

This story has elements particularly important for consideration with middle school children. Not only is it important for them to understand persons with communication and hearing problems but it is important to understand the importance of protecting their hearing throughout life. They also are beginning to think about career possibilities.

Discuss experiences the children have had with hearing impaired people. Present information about hearing impairment found in the section about disabilities. Discuss experiences they may have had with temporary hearing loss. You may find it appropriate to talk briefly about some of the ways people can protect their ears from being damaged.

You may tell them that Jimmy, in today's story, was born deaf.

Read: WHEN I GROW UP.

Discussion:

¤ What questions did Jimmy have about growing up?

¤ How did Jimmy communicate with his mother?

¤ What problems might Jimmy have if he came to your school? How could you communicate with him?

¤ What might you have to do to learn to 'talk' with him?

¤ Jimmy's mother told him he had to work on his speech. What do you think that means for him?

¤ In what ways might you expect Jimmy's speaking to be strange sounding to us?

¤ Jimmy wondered about what he would do when he grew up. Take a few moments to share questions and concerns they may have had about future careers.

SUGGESTED ACTIVITIES

Learn Some of the Signs

Divide the group into pairs. assign certain words to each group. Practice the signs. Re-read the story, signing at the appropriate places.

Make a List

Divide into small groups.

Have each group make a list of one of the following topics:

      PLEASANT SOUNDS I LIKE TO HEAR

      WARNING SOUNDS I MUST HEAR

      THINGS I CAN DO TO PROTECT MY HEARING

      THINGS I CAN SHARE WITH JIMMY WITHOUT WORDS

      Share the lists for discussion. Discuss how important it is to protect hearing and the consequences as they relate to the lists.

Write a Poem

      Write a poem, using words and signs, about something you would like to do when you grow up. Use some of the signs found in WHEN I GROW UP. Research other words you might want to use and sign to express your ideas. Share the poems when finished.

NOTES

53

THE NIGHT SEARCH

OBJECTIVE: through story and discussion:
- ¤ to increase awareness and understanding of lifestyle and feelings of persons who are blind
- ¤ to become aware of the ways in which we are similar

FOR KINDERGARTEN CHILDREN

Discussion before reading the story:
- ¤ Who has been camping? What did you see?
- ¤ Now, everyone close your eyes. What do you hear (and smell)? What are some things you hear and smell when you go camping?

Today we are going to read a story about a little girl who cannot see. She likes to go camping just as you do. And, when she goes camping, she uses her ears (listens) and nose (smells) to help her get around.

Read: THE NIGHT SEARCH

Discussion after reading the story:
- ¤ What was the little girl's name? What was her puppy's name?
- ¤ Who has a pet just like Heather? Tell us about your pet.
- ¤ Heather was blind. What does it mean to be blind?
- ¤ Why did she go outside during the night?
- ¤ What happened when she went to the bathroom?
- ¤ What happened to her as she tried to find Crackers?
- ¤ Have you ever lost something like Heather did? Te ll us about it.
- ¤ What were the night sounds that she heard? Where did she find Crackers?
- ¤ What were the things she smelled or heard as she walked to the pond?
- ¤ What did she find that helped her to walk back to her tent?
- ¤ Do you think she will take her cane next time she goes for a walk? Why or why not?
- ¤ Do you know someone like Heather? Tell us about them.

SUGGESTED ACTIVITIES
Pretend Camping Trip

Pretend you are going on a camping trip. Read the story inside a tent with pine twigs spread around or read the story outdoors. While on your camping trip, eat lunch outside on your sleeping bags (or mats). Have all the children blindfolded (or close their eyes) during lunch. Ask them to describe what they are having for lunch while blindfolded.

What Do We Smell

Blind fold each child or have them close their eyes and find their way to the snack time after the story using their sense of smell. Along the way place fragrant objects to help them (i.e.,flowers; ripe or cut fruit such as lemons, bananas; fresh popcorn; pine twigs; etc.)

What Do We Hear

Have children identify objects from story while they are blind-folded (or have their eyes closed). Encourage them to use their sense of touch and hearing. Examples of objects for touching might include: pan of water, a cane, a sleeping bag, a pine cone or twig Examples of objects for hearing might include: crackling leaves, dripping water, cane clicking the pavement, rattle of a dog collar, dog barking, walking feet, singing, hooting owl.

FOR ELEMENTARY CHILDREN

You may discuss disabilities in general and conditions causing blindness. They may have older relatives who are visually impaired or legally blind. Answer any questions or share experiences they may have had.

Ask how many have ever been camping. Talk about what they take if they go overnight, with a group or with their families. Tell them that today they are going to hear a story about Heather, who is blind. She also enjoys going camping with her family.

Read: THE NIGHT SEARCH

Discussion:
   ¤ What did Heather want to leave behind when she went to camp? Why do you suppose she didn't want to take it?
   ¤ Discuss some of the problems she might have experienced with the cane that made her feel uncomfortable about taking it.
   ¤ What do you take to help you when you go out for a walk at night? What might happen if you decided not to take a flashlight?
   ¤ Recall some of the experiences Heather had in her search for Crackers.
   ¤ Why did she wish she had her cane?
   ¤ Why was the return trip easier?
   ¤ What did the sunbeam show when it peeped through the tent flap?

SUGGESTED ACTIVITIES
Eat a Snack
    Blind fold each child or have them close their eyes. Place a paper plate in front of each child. On each plate arrange several small pieces of food having different textures and odors. Have each child pick up and identify each item before tasting it. You might wish to keep score to see who could identify the most items without tasting. You might use chunks of banana, squares of bread and peanut butter, orange and apple slices, chocolate chip cookie, marshmallow, raw potato or small pieces of pizza. (Check for food allergies before preparing the snack.)

Listening
    Prepare a tape containing various sounds such as: a ticking clock, a bird or cricket, a toilet flushing, a refrigerator door shutting, a car driving away, a cat purring, a newspaper being opened, etc. You may use a sound effects record or tape as a resource when you make your tape. Have the children sit quietly and listen. "What do you hear? Can you identify the sounds?"
    You may find it helpful to use a sound effects record or tape as a resource when you make your tape for class. Such recordings may be available at your local library or record shop.

Invite a Guest
    Invite a person who is blind and uses a guide dog to come and talk with your group. You may wish to discuss the trip with the children before the visit to find their questions and interests. Then prepare a few questions for the guest to have before the session. (check for animal allergies before bringing in the dog.)

FOR MIDDLE SCHOOL

    Briefly discuss disabilities in general and some causes of blindness. Many middle school children may have had experiences with visually impaired older persons. Allow time to discuss these experiences. Talk about some of the vision problems they may have. These problems may not cause blindness but certainly can interfere with school work if not corrected with glasses or contact lenses.
    Before reading the story tell them that, though Heather is blind, she is very much like each of them in many ways. She gets herself into a difficult situation on a camping trip. Listen and decide how you feel about how she solves the problem.

Read: THE NIGHT SEARCH

Discussion:

- How did Heather feel about her cane?
- Why did she think she wouldn't need it?
- Have any of you gone camping with a group or with your family?
- Have you ever been out in the woods alone at night? What did you take to help you?
- Have you ever left the flashlight behind and tried to walk a familiar path in the dark? How did you feel?
- Why was the return trip easier?
- Recall some of the ways she used the stick to help avoid trouble.
- How did her feelings for her cane change? How do we know?

SUGGESTED ACTIVITIES

You may prefer to use some of the activities from the elementary plan.

Simulate Low-vision

Have the children make and "wear" one or more of the following:

- low-vision simulators made from two thicknesses of wax paper or quilted plastic bag (basic light perception) You might make them from pieces of cardboard with wax paper "lenses". Hold them in place like swim goggles with a length of elastic.
- tunnel vision: use cardboard with a small hole cut in the middle, similar to the glasses suggested above.
- macular degeneration-blacken a circle in the middle of clear plastic in the glasses above.
- total blindness- blindfold

Trust Walk

Blindfold one child. The blind-folded child takes the arm of the guide, who is another child who is not blind folded. The guide is to talk the first child through without touching him or her.

Cane Travel

This activity may be adapted for kindergarten and elementary students.

Borrow an appropriate sized white cane or use a dowel. The cane should be approximately long enough to reach the sternum. Have the children take turns walking with eyes closed or blind-folded, using the cane. The rest of the class might sing-song the words on page 23. It may be advisable to have someone walk with the child to help guide as needed. (You may wish to practice first using the following suggestions before blind-folding.)

The length of the cane is determined by the forward stepping motion of the person using it. It should extend an inch or two ahead of the forward stepping motion. The child extends the right arm, wrist bent to allow the cane to cross the body. Right foot is forward. The left is behind. The cane taps the spot ahead of the left foot where the left foot will land on the next forward step.When the left foot comes forward it appears to kick the cane over to the right side. The right side then kicks it back to the left, etc.

Note: As a follow-on study, you may wish to read and discuss the story "Polka Dot Birthday Map" by Kathy Kennedy Tapp found on page 82.

"HOW-TO"

ROLE PLAY

Role play is the acting out of a situation by members of the group to help the players and the group develop insight, understand feelings or help solve a problem. The players use spontaneous dialog and pantomime.

Role play allows children to pretend to be another person. It allows them to explore ways to solve a problem. They may come to realize that their own feelings are not unique. They may be able to re-live an awkward experience trying for a happier ending.

Use role play in brief time periods but always allow enough time for discussion of insights and feelings. You may wish to use simple props or costumes such as hats, scarves, chairs, eating utensils.

PLAN

Decide on the situation and objective to be hoped for. Gather any props. Decide how you will present the situation to the children, get the action moving and keep it on track. Plan how you will bring the children back to themselves and the classroom after the action stops.

PLAY

¤ Establish the situation with the children. Set the scene, the problem, the characters.

¤ Select the players from volunteers if possible. Emphasize that the rest of the group are viewers and will be involved in discussion.

¤ Play the scene. End it when the action is strong, and the objective has been accomplished. End by interrupting and announcing that the role play has ended, the players are once again themselves. Call them by name to return to their seats.

FOLLOW UP

Talk about the experience. Include viewers and players in discussion. Discuss possible new insights, understandings, feelings, skills. Discuss things they like or things they might wish to have done differently. You may even wish to try it again with another cast if time permits and the children are not satisfied with the outcome.

MURAL

A mural is a large surface containing many pictures centering around a single theme or telling a story.

If the room size permits, the children may work together on the floor using one long sheet of paper. If that is not possible each child can work independently on a smaller sheet of paper which will be taped in a pre-planned sequence into one long picture.

Making a mural encourages children to share individual ideas that may become part of a larger subject or idea.

The pictures may be made of brown paper in rolls or newsprint from an end roll from a newspaper printing shop, sheets of brown wrapping paper or newsprint sheets. Crayons, tempera paints, and felt markers make satisfactory murals.

PLAN

Plan subjects that might interest the children. Decide what will be used to draw with and on. Collect all supplies including papers or drop cloth to cover the floor if you will be using paints. Decide how you will direct the project to ensure that everyone will share and that the activity will fit into the time slot you have alloted.

DO A MURAL

Help the children decide from the discussion period what they wish to include in the mural.

If you are using a long sheet of paper, divide the class into small groups ready to work on each section. Divide the paper into sections with chalk lines. Write with chalk on each section what the contents of that section will be. From the group working on each section, decide who will work on the background, the animals, buildings, people, etc. It may be wise to have the children sketch in chalk before color is added.

This activity is quite time consuming when using a single piece of paper and working as a group. Making individual pictures taped together isn't a true mural, but it is much faster and more manageable as far as time and classroom order is concerned.

FOLLOW UP

Discuss the learnings. Plan to hang the mural or share with another class the picture and the learnings.

MONTAGE

Montage is a collection of individual pictures arranged to form one large picture having a common theme or central idea. Making a montage can be a valuable learning experience as the children sort through photographs or magazines evaluating and choosing for the common theme.

PREPARE

Gather magazine pictures, photos, catalogs, newspapers. Provide poster board, glue or paste, scissors, black felt marker (to outline the individual pictures after they are pasted.) If, as you collect pictures, you select and tear only pertinent pictures, it will save class time.

PLAN

Through discussion, decide on the theme and how they might want it pictured. You may wish to divide into work groups selecting, cutting, arranging and pasting. Perhaps it would be easier and quicker for each group of 6 or 7 children to make one montage.

FOLLOW UP

Share and discuss the finished montage. Talk about how well it fits the theme and expresses the desired learning.

SIMULATION

Simulation is a teaching tool to help children experience and understand a specific problem or situation. As children assume the role of another person, they begin to understand some of the feelings, elements involved and consequences in real life situations. Simulation differs from role play in that it may involve the entire group in the action rather than single players. True simulations are best with older children. Simple simulations may be used very effectively with young children, however.

PLAN

Create the simulation situation, thinking through how you expect it to achieve the objective. Plan the directions you will be giving to the children. Collect any props or materials. "Walk through" it mentally or act it out with two or three people. Write out evaluation and discussion questions for the post-play period.

PLAY

Give the group specific instructions for the play. Direct as needed to lead them through the simulation.

FOLLOW-UP

When the action has reached the experience hoped for, announce that the play is over. Direct them back to their seats, using their real names.

At this point you, as director, are ready to use your evaluation discussion questions. Talk together about the experience and any changes in attitudes, feelings or concepts that may have taken place.

A WORD ABOUT THE SENSITIZING EXPERIENCES

These activities have been gathered over the years and used to help people without disabilities feel a little of the difficulties and frustrations faced by individuals with disabilities on a daily basis. They can't fully create the experiences because people without disabilities can stop the activities whenever they wish, but it's a start.

These activities were used as weekly homework activities for college students. The experiences can be used "as is" for teenagers and adults. Some may not be appropriate for use with children as they may be too threatening. However, by adjusting the time spent or the number of activities done at one time, many can be successfully used with children starting at grades three or four.

They can be shortened and adapted to a "station format" for a day-long workshop. Each station would have an instruction stand and materials. For example:

AREA OF NEED: ORTHOPEDIC

PROCEDURE: Wrap a post-it note around a marker.
Hold it in your mouth.
Write your name.
Draw a figure.

When you are finished, please throw the note paper away.
Materials needed: thin markers
self stick notes
paper to write on

SENSITIZING EXPERIENCES

It is often difficult for a person without special needs to imagine how it feels to be disabled in some way. The following activities help make a person aware of some of the difficulties faced by many of our fellow human beings.

Many of these experiences may be used with children by shortening the time involved or simplifying the activity. They would be especially valuable to help children prepare for receiving children with disabilities into their homes or class rooms.

BLINDNESS

EXPERIMENT 1.

For one hour, be in your home blindfolded. Try to make the blindfold lightproof. Do this at a time that will overlap a meal, including preparation and clean-up.

Some questions to think about:

1. Can you tell who is talking to whom?
2. Can you find the food on your plate?
3. Can you walk easily around the house?
4. Can you wash dishes?
5. Can you put things away?
6. Can you tell what you are holding?
7. Does food taste the same?

EXPERIMENT 2.

For one hour, cover your eyes with quilted type "baggies". This creates blurry vision. If you develop a headache, stop.

Some questions to think about.

1. Can you clearly distinguish objects?
2. Can you read?
3. Can you watch television?
4. What muscles of your face are being used that you never noticed before?
5. Can you see small things on the floor?

EXPERIMENT 3.

Take a red and blue gel (the assignment covers sold in stationary stores are fine) and make a shield for your eyes. It will be dark purple. Wear it for one hour during the evening. If you develop a headache, stop.

Some questions to think about:

1. Can you read?
2. Can you distinguish shadow?
3. Can you watch television from a distance?
4. Can you see out of the window?

EXPERIMENT 4.

Try to obtain an adhesive eye patch. For one hour, wear the eyepatch, making sure that you cannot see with the patched eye. This experiment spoils your binocular vision. Although you may not realize it, you are only seeing in two dimensions. Your apparent ability to see depth is only present because you understand depth and expect it to be there. You are able to judge familiar surroundings. If you only had the use of one eye from birth, you would not understand depth visually and to your view, everything would appear flat.

If possible, also try this experiment outside, in a shopping mall or some other large area. Go up and down a flight of stairs. DO NOT DRIVE.

Some questions to think about:

1. Can you pour from a pitcher into a narrow necked bottle when it is near you? when an arm's length away?
2. Can you judge how far away people are in a long corridor?
3. Do you stumble going downstairs?
4. How steep do the stairs look from the top:?

EXPERIMENT 5.

Pass around a Braille card. Students should feel the dots with their fingers and try to distinguish one letter from another. That will be hard enough. Then have them run their fingers along a line with some speed, as people usually read. They will realize how difficult it is to learn Braille and how unsensitive their touch is since that skill is not needed.

DEAFNESS

EXPERIMENT 1.

Watch a one-half hour situation comedy or drama on television with the sound completely off.

Questions to think about:
1. Could you follow the plot properly?
2. Did some actions appear meaningless?
3. Was all the humor apparent?
4. Was it easier to understand when actors faced the camera?
5. On what did you find yourself concentrating?
6. Did you get bored?

EXPERIMENT 2.

Buy a set of wax ear plugs. Wear them for one hour. If hearing is not sufficiently dull, use ear muffs, too. Do this experiment during a meal or at a time when the family is interacting. If possible, make a phone call at some time. Question to think about.
1. Could you follow the conversation around you?
2. Did people exclude you from their conversations?
3. Were you able to converse naturally on the phone?
4. Did you find yourself shouting?
5. Did people get angry trying to make you understand?
6. Did you find the experience frustrating?
7. Could you hear TV set for everyone else's comfort?

CEREBRAL PALSY

EXPERIMENT 1.

Wrap a student's legs securely from hip to knee (a simple tie is not enough). Have the student walk around the room. This demonstrates the scissors gait.

EXPERIMENT 2.

Stand two students side by side. Securely wrap their inside legs together from hip to ankle. Give one a set of directions for walking around certain objects, going left or right, etc. They may not talk to each other. This demonstrates being unable to predict what half of you will do.

EXPERIMENT 3.

Have student do a two-handed task, such as a kindergarten type weaving project, while wearing a gardening glove on the dominant hand. This demonstrates Hemiplegia.

EXPERIMENT 4.

Use a rocker board of large circle of plywood to which a hub cap has been attached. Have a student stand on it wearing a man's shirt. Have the student button the shirt as you rock the board. This demonstrates balance problems.

EXPERIMENT 5.

Hold a pencil in your dominant hand while making a fist. Tense all your muscles and write your name. This demonstrates spasticity.

EXPERIMENT 6.

Chew 5 packages of bubble gum at one time. Read a story aloud with all the gum in your mouth. This demonstrates speech problems with mouth muscle involvement.

Questions to think about:

    1. Are activities frustrating? embarrassing?

    2. Do you feel clumsy? awkward? conspicuous? foolish? on display?

    3. Was it a relief to stop the activity? Suppose you couldn't?

LANGUAGE

EXPERIMENT

For an entire day, do not speak. You must do this for a full day to get the impact of being unable to communicate verbally. Do as little as possible for yourself. Try instead, to communicate your needs to others. Do not write.

Questions to think about:

    1. Was your experience frustrating?

    2. Did your acting ability improve throughout the day?

    3. How did you feel when people looked at you?

    4. How did you feel when people did not look at you?

    5. How did children react to you?

    6. Did people include you in their conversations?

BRAIN DAMAGE

EXPERIMENT

Use the mirror mazes found at the end of this section for this experiment.

Two people work at this activity together. You need a mirror, about 8 inches by 10 inches or larger, and a firm cardboard about the same size. One person sits looking into the mirror with the maze paper in front of him or her. The person places a pencil point at start. The second person then positions the cardboard so that the first person can only see the maze in the mirror. Person One then tries to stay within the path of the top design, and tries to stay on the line in the second. Then the partners switch. The entire class should do this activity before discussion. It is also interesting to try it using the non-dominant hand. Questions to think about:

1. Is this activity easy?
2. What happened when your eye told you one thing and your mind wanted you to do something else?
3. Did you ever become immobilized so you could not move on, but kept going over and over the same spot?
4. Was it frustrating to do?
5. Did you get annoyed or angry when you couldn't stay on the line?

The teacher can add to the problems by making comments such as:

"What's the matter? It's a simple line. Surely you can follow a line. I told you not to go outside the line. Look at that big space you have for your pencil...still you are sloppy."

Draw comparisons with kindergarten teachers and some coloring projects.

RETARDATION

This is the hardest disability to demonstrate. You can't make a person with above average intelligence unable to learn. However, it is possible to make that person feel stupid, dull, and chagrinned about his or her abilities by using puzzles and games with unexpected components.

Most of the following puzzle can be done by anyone given enough time, energy and above all, patience.

LETTER PUZZLES

These are wonderful because they show up interesting individual behaviors and also give insight into how the brain works.

METHOD

Announce that you are going to give the class an important psychological test. They are not to look at anyone else or talk about the paper. They may begin as soon as they get the paper. Place a paper on each desk.

At first many will give the paper a blank stare. Some may nervously laugh as they realize that they can't understand anything on it. Some will think it is a joke and give up, putting down their pencils and gazing at the ceiling. When some people start writing, they will look confused and may or may not try to deal with their papers again. Those who manage to start often appear smug as they realize that others are not writing. After 10 minutes, have everyone stop. Ask how many have answered 1 question, 1 to 5 questions, 5 to 10 and more than 10. Tell them to write "session 1" and the number completed, at the bottom of the page and to put the papers away. After 30 to 45 minutes, have them work on the papers for another 10 minutes. The brain has worked on the problems during the time since the last attempt, and many students who had not solved any before, will begin to solve them now. At the end of the 10 minutes, take another poll and have the students write "session 2" and the number solved at the bottom of the page.

Tell the students to take the puzzles home and work on them for 15 minutes a day without consulting anyone else, and to bring them back for the next session. At the next session, go over the answers and take a final poll.

1. Discuss student's feelings during the first session - anger? frustration? feeling stupid (especially when seeing others writing)? mad at teacher for giving out the papers, etc.

2. Discuss different responses-reading the paper over and over, reading the first question over and over, giving up right away, etc.

3. Compare totals of students who got answers right away and those who didn't. It often makes no difference in the final total.

4. See if people had answers pop into their heads at odd times-middle of the night-at supper-whatever.

5. Was it easier as soon as they got one answer? Compare which were the first questions to be answered by different students.

6. How many got so fixated on the idea that this was math, that they could not get started for a long time?

7. Point up the differences in people: the ones who gave up, the ones who kept trying, the ones who acted superior, the ones who tried to look at other student's papers. Then remind students that they are all in a capable, intelligent people regardless of their abilities on this test.

This paper is one of the few that lets a person feel really stupid. Since many children with special needs have occasion to feel many of the feelings the students feel during this exercise, it is especially valuable.

LETTER PUZZLE

1. M. + M. + N.H. + V. + C. + R.I. = N.E.
2. "1B. IN THE H. = 2 IN THE <u>B</u>".
3. 8D. - 24H. = 1W.
4. H.H. + M.H. at 12 = N. or M.
5. 3P. = 6
6. 4J. + 4Q. + 4K. = all the F.C.
7. S. + M. + T. + W. + T. + F. + S are D of W
8. A. + N. + A.F. + M.C. + C.G. = A.F.
9. T. = L.S. State
10. 23Y. - 3Y. = 2D.
11. E. - 8 = Z.
12. 8P. = 1G.
13 C. + 6D. = N.Y.E.
14. S.R. of N. = 3
15 A. and E. were in the G. of E.
16. My F.L. and South P. are both M.C.
17. "N.N. = G.N."
18. N. + P. + S.M. = S. of C.
19. 1 + 6Z = 1M.
20. B. or G. - F. - M. = O
21. "R. - R. = R."
22. A.L. + J.G. + W.M. + J. K. were all A.
23. N. + V. + P. + A. + A. + C. + P. + I. = P. of S.
24. S. + H. of R. = U.S.C.
25. P. + N. + D. + Q. + H.D. are all C.
26. Y. = S. + S + -A. + W
27 Y. + 2D. = T.
28. O. + Y. + V. + R + G. + B. = R.
29 2H. + O. = W.
30. "D. = G.B.F."
31. C. + s. + T. + R. + D. = S.
32. W. + B. + P. + S. = O
33. 4 x 20 + 7 = G.A.
34. 6 o. = 1 i.
35. D. + R. + M. + F. + S. + L. + T. + D. = S.
36. O.T.T.F.F.S.S.___

ANSWERS

1. Maine+Massachusetts+New Hampshire+Vermont+Connecticut+Rhode Island= New England
2. A bird in the hand = two in the bush.
3. 8 days minus 24 hours = 1 week
4. hour hand and minute hand at 12 = noon or midnight
5. 3 pairs = 6
6. 4 Jacks + 4 Queens + 4 Kings = all the face cards
7. Sun., Mon, Tues, Wed, Thurs, Fri, Sat are days of the week
8. Army, Navy, Air Force, Marine Corps + Coast Guard = Armed Forces
9. Texas is the Lone Star State
10. 23 years - 3 years = 2 decades
11. Eight - 8= Zero
12. 8 pints = 1 Gallon
13. Christmas + 6 days= New Years Eve
14. Square root of 9=3
15. Adam and Eve were in the Garden of Eden
16. My Fair Lady and South Pacific are Musical Comedies
17. No News= Good News
18. Nina + Pinta +Santa Maria= Ships of Columbus
19. 1 + 6 zeros=1 million
20. Boy or Girl-female-male=0
21. Rose is a rose is a rose
22. Abe Lincoln+James Garfield+Wm. McKinley+John Kennedy -assassinated.
23. Noun,verb,pronoun,adverb,adjective,conjunction,preposition,interjection= parts of speech
24. Senate+ House of Representatives=United States Congress
25. Penny,nickel,dime.quarter, half dollar are all coins or currency
26. Year=Spring+Summer+Autumn+Winter
27. Yesterday + 2days=tomorrow
28. Orange,yellow, violet, red, green ,blue= rainbow
29. H_2O= water
30. Diamonds are a girl's best friend
31. Circle ,square,triangle,rectangle, diamond=shapes
32. Woodwinds, brass, percussion, strings = orchestra
33. 4 score +7= Gettysburg Address
34. 6 outs = 1 inning
35. Do,re, mi, fa sol, la, ti, do= scale
36. 1 2 3 4 5 6 7 <u>8</u>

ASSORTED CATEGORIES TO HEIGHTEN AWARENESS

This activity is to heighten awareness of how people react to others under specific conditions. The success of this activity depends upon the personalities of the group. If people won't mix together and talk, it won't work. If this can be done during a break, when coffee and snack can be served, the students will be less self-conscious and it will work better. ***Do not use those with* with children.***

METHOD

Make headbands for each student, choosing ideas from the following list: or inventing your own ideas. Place a headband on each person but do not allow that person to see what it says. Instruct the class to treat all classmates as if what the headband they are wearing says is true, or to follow the instructions on the headband if it is written in instruction form. Let everyone mingle freely for 10 or 15 minutes. Then have everyone sit down.

1. Ask students if they can figure out what their headbands say. After they guess, they may look.

2. Ask students how they felt during this exercise. Many answers are interesting and revealing.

3. Relate the headband to a type of special needs child or situation that might occur in a classroom.

HEADBAND IDEAS

*1. I do everything wrong
 2. Be kind to me.
 3. Tell me to talk more slowly. I am hard to understand.
*4. My nose is dripping.
 5. I can't hear you.
 6. Treat me like the most popular person here.
 7. You can't understand me.
 8. Try to find out about me.
*9. I look funny. (Odd-Strange)
*10. Ignore me.
 11. I don't look healthy.
 12. I am very pretty.
 13. Ask me about my family and friends but don't ask about me.
*14. Act as if I have something catching.
 15. When you talk to me, don't look at me.
 16. I don't pay attention when you talk.
 17. Keep telling me not to worry.
 18. Treat me as if I behave very strangely.
*19. Tell me that I'll do better if I try harder.
*20. Don't talk to me.

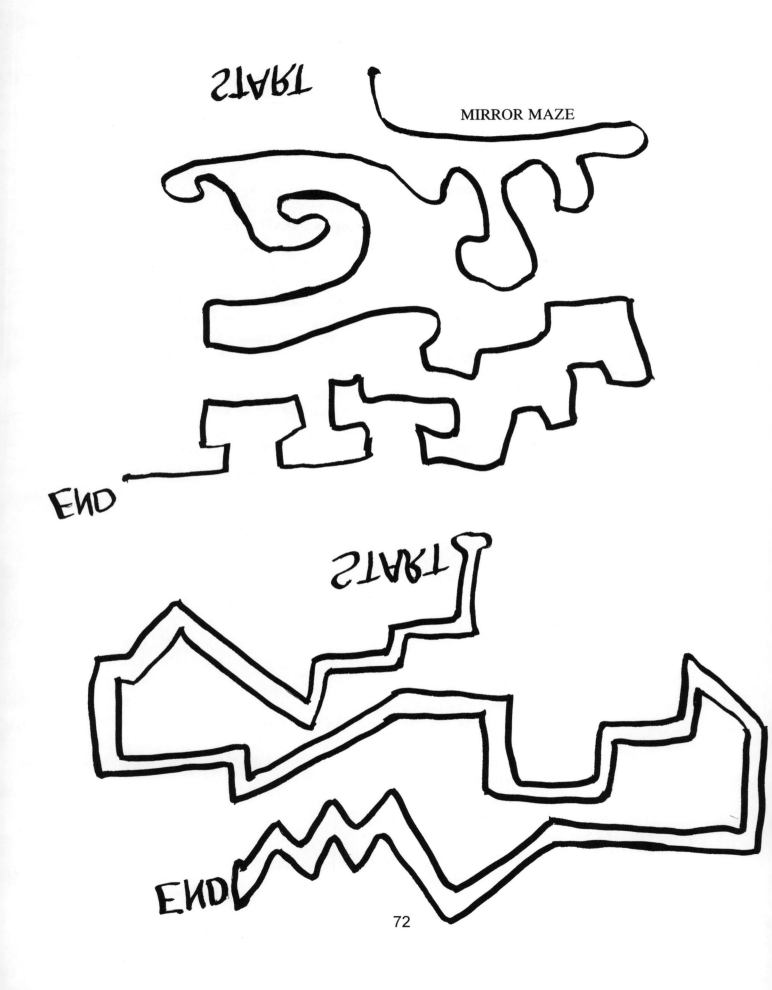

MIRROR MAZE

72

JUST FOR FUN STORIES

The following stories are just for fun. You may wish to develop your own discussion questions and activities to use with them. They are particularly suited for use with preschool children. The characters may be found in other TURTLE BOOKS.

THE BEST FACE OF ALL
By Nan Holcomb

Andy swallowed the last bit of chocolate pudding and watched his mother's smiling face as she washed the pudding from his chin with a cold, wet washcloth. He felt like yelling good and loud. He hated having his face washed but he knew he couldn't go for a walk with a dirty face.

Soon he was strapped into his chair, bumped down the steps and they were on their way. "If I didn't have my face, maybe I wouldn't have to have it washed so much," he thought as he rolled along. Just then he saw a small black dog with shaggy hair all over its face.

"I could have a black hairy face and the pudding wouldn't show," he thought.

"How do you like that hairy face?" Mom asked. "You'd have to have a hair cut on your chin if you looked like that."

"A haircut on my chin?" Andy thought. That sounds worse than a cold wet washcloth.

They walked on until they came to a gas station. There a little car was getting its windshield washed.

"I could have a car face," Andy thought.

"See, the car's getting a face wash," Mom said. "You'd have bugs in your teeth if you had a car face."

"I don't want a car face," Andy thought as he watched the dirty sponge drop into the bucket. A cold sponge on a stick must feel a lot worse than a cold, wet washcloth.

As they started home, a policeman rode up on his beautiful brown horse. He smiled at Andy.

"Would you like to pet the horse?" he asked. Andy was so excited he started to shake all over. The policeman held the horse's face down so Andy could touch the smooth brown hair.

"Isn't that soft?" the policeman asked. "I rub him down every morning with a wire brush." That sounded worse than a sponge on a stick or a haircut and much worse than a cold, wet washcloth.

"Thank you," Andy's mother said to the policeman and they walked on. Soon they bumped up the steps and into the hall. There in the mirror Andy saw his very own face. He smiled and his face smiled back. I guess I have the best face of all, he thought. Even if it does get washed with a cold, wet washcloth.

THE BEST COOKIE EATER IN TOWN
By Nan Holcomb

Molly loved cookies:big brown molasses cookies, little fancy pink cookies, chewy chocolate drops or even plain oatmeal cookies. Molly loved them all.

Molly bounced up and down on her chair and clapped her hands when the teacher said, "Boys and girls, we're going to have a Christmas cookie party."

Molly shut her eyes and pictured gingerbread men sitting on a pile of chocolate chip cookies. Santa cookies were running around chasing reindeer cookies. Best of all, Molly saw herself sitting in the middle of the floor eating them all. Until...the teacher said, "We're going to bake the cookies and pack them in boxes."

Molly couldn't believe what Miss Wills said next.

"And...we'll take them to the nursing home so the old people can eat the cookies we have made." Old people eating her beautiful gingerbread men sitting on the huge pile of chocolate chip cookies?

"But why?" Molly thought as she watched Miss Wills roll the dough.

"But why?" Molly thought as she pressed the cookie cutter into the dough and watched Miss Wills put it onto the cookie sheet.

"But why?" she thought as she helped the other children poke raisins in the icing for eyes and sprinkled colored sugar over the top.

Molly didn't smile as she and the other children held boxes of cookies and rode through the countryside to the old peoples home. She didn't smile when the helpers unloaded Patrick's walker and Danny's chair and helped them up the walk. She didn't smile when an old man took her arm and helped her up the ramp just like walking the balance beam at school. She didn't smile when they all were pushed together in an elevator and carried up, up, up to a huge sunny room.

Molly looked around the room and smiled a big smile. There on the table were the cookies they'd made and lots of cookies someone else had made. In the middle of the table was a huge punch bowl filled with red punch and green ice.A huge Christmas tree stood in the center of the room.

Suddenly, Molly heard bells and a voice calling, "Ho,ho,ho!" She looked up and there came Santa riding in a wheel chair.

"Merry Christmas! Happy Holidays!" people called to each other.

An old lady in a walker like Patrick's, only bigger, held out her hand to Molly. "Welcome to our party, little girl. It's so nice of you to come and help us celebrate. Did you make some of those cookies?"

Molly felt so happy and proud. She smiled and nodded, then said,"Yes."

"And are you a good cookie eater?" the woman asked.

"The best cookie eater in town," Molly answered and smiled the biggest smile around.

DANNY AND THE IVY

By Nan Holcomb

One plant in Danny's living room made him very cross. Actually Danny decided one morning he hated that plant. It wasn't the palm in the corner. It wasn't the plant with the yellow spots on the leaves. It wasn't the violet with the soft velvety leaves and purple flowers. It was the hanging ivy in front of the big window. It had been hanging there as long as Danny could remember. Every day Danny had grown bigger and every day the branches of the plant had grown longer.

Every day Danny's mother wheeled him to the window to watch for his sister's school bus. The ivy hung over the edge of the pot above his head. Danny looked up and the leaves looked down.

One spring day Danny looked up and the leaves brushed his hair. Danny moved his head. By summer Danny looked up and the leaves tickled his nose. He crossed his eyes and looked around it.

In the fall Danny couldn't see past the ivy at all. Something had to be done. Danny opened his teeth and grabbed a leaf. He pulled and tugged and tugged and pulled. Finally he could see through a little hole.

By Christmas new leaves had filied the hole.

"That plant has got to go," Danny thought. "But how? That's what I'd like to know." He'd like to take it down, or pull it down or cut it off or break it off or tell it NOT TO GROW!

But I can't. My arms don't work well enough to do any of those things. He glared at the ivy. The ivy didn't glare back. It looks kind of pretty, Danny thought. And that's a fact. But it just has to go!

Danny peered into the ivy. "If I could move my arms the right way, but..." then a voice inside Danny said, "Go ahead. Give it a try!" So Danny thought very hard, then inch by inch, he reached for a branch with his best hand and brought his hand back as fast as he could. The branch fell at his feet.

Danny smiled and then, inch by inch, he reached for another and down it went. Soon the ivy no longer covered his face, or tickled his nose or brushed on his hair. The ivy lay all around his chair. Just then his mother came in and said, "Now who did that!" Danny first looked sad and then he looked glad.

Mommy said, "It needed a trim, I must admit. But now it looks like it had been run over by a bulldozer." She picked up the branches. Danny tried not to grin. "Don't feel bad, Danny. It'll grow back and each of these branches will grow another plant. Won't that be grand?" Danny looked up and groaned.

Now when Danny sits by the window and waits for his sister, he looks around twelve ivy plants hanging all around and he thinks to himself, "I can do a lot more than I think I can! Maybe they'll call me 'Dan, the ivy man.'"

DANNY TAKES A SPECIAL WALK
By Nan Holcomb

"I have a surprise for you today, Danny," Mom said, as she strapped him into his chair and bumped him down the steps. "I'm going shopping and Brian is going to keep you company. How do you like that idea?"

"Hi, Hot Wheels!" Brian called. Danny grinned at Brian. Brian always called him something funny, like 'rabbit-nose' or 'super-spud'. Danny liked hot wheels the best.

"I hope you're ready for the walk of your life," Brian said and pushed Danny quickly around in a circle. Danny giggled. His mother just pushed the chair to get from one place to another. Brian made it go fast, go slow, circle and back up, weave in and out until Danny felt like a bird or a train. Sometimes when his mother wasn't around, Brian ran as fast as he could. Danny waved his arms with excitement. He could hardly wait to get to the park.

"Not so fast, Super Sox," Brian said. "This isn't going to be your ordinary walk in the park. On this walk you're going to learn to see." Brian pushed the chair hard and Danny rolled ahead of him almost like running up the street.

"See? I know how to see," Danny thought. "I may not walk and I may not talk but I can see!"

Suddenly the chair stopped in front of a concrete wall. Brian turned the chair and pushed Danny up so his nose nearly touched the concrete. "Now what do you see?"

Danny looked and looked. Then he rolled his eyes up at Brian and shook his head.

"Very good. There wasn't anything to see except grey concrete wall. Maybe you'll learn to see very quickly," Brian said and pushed on.

Soon they met Danny's friend, the policeman with the horse. "Good morning, Danny," the policeman said. "Would you like to pet my horse today?"

Danny smiled and raised his hand. The horse gently nudged Danny with his nose and Danny opened his hand. Then the horse poked Danny, ever so gently and raised his head, ready to walk on.

"Thank you," Brian called and the policeman waved his hand. "What did you see?"

"A horse," Danny thought and looked puzzled.

"Did you see his eyelashes?" Brian asked. "Horses do have eyelashes. Or, did you see the way his lip curled up and showed big yellow teeth?"

Danny smiled. He did see the teeth. They were pretty scary that close to his nose.

"Good. Not great, but good." Brian started to run. Danny laughed hard.

They fairly flew into the park. Then Brian stopped quickly. Danny thought he might fly right out of his chair.

"Shh-h-h, we'll wait here." Brian crouched down and they waited and watched. Then Brian poked Danny and pointed. There by the tree, as close as could be sat a fat grey squirrel with a nut in its paws. Danny's eyes grew wide. He reached out his hand. The squirrel flicked his tail, popped the nut in his mouth and ran up the tree. Danny laughed.

"Well, what did you see? What kind of a nut did it have?"

"Nut?" Danny thought. He shrugged and thought. I don't know. I didn't see.

"An acorn. See that tree? That's an oak tree and these are acorns. The squirrel could see the nuts on the tree. Look up and see!"

Danny looked up and saw the tree, the leaves, the blue sky and just then something made a chattering sound and an acorn hit Danny on the chest.

Brian laughed. "I guess it's time to go. That was the squirrel. He threw the nut and told us it was time to go home."

Danny watched the squirrel bound from branch to branch and waved and laughed as Brian whirled his chair around. They dashed up the path, crossed the corner by the concrete wall and soon they were bumping up the steps into the hall.

"Did you have a good walk?" Mom asked as she unfastened the straps on his chair.

He looked over her shoulder and saw himself in the mirror. He saw his eyelashes, his own white teeth and he smiled.

"The best," he thought. A learning-to-see walk was the best of all walks.

PEER BUDDIES: I CAN HELP

By Judith J. Foil

One day Mr. Mistretta told our class we had a new first grader. Her name was Lauren, and he told us she would need peer buddies to spend extra time with her. When he asked for helpers, I raised my hand. "I can help," I said, "I know I can."

That afternoon when it was time for centers, Mr. Mistretta chose me to sit with Lauren. She was six, just like me, but when she talked, I didn't know what she said.

"Why doesn't she talk right?" I asked.

"Lauren has Down syndrome. It's hard for her," he answered.

"But, I could say `MaMa' when I was one."

"Lauren is slower. She didn't say `MaMa' until she was four."

"My little sister is four, and she says all kinds of stuff. I know I can make Lauren talk. I can help."

"Lauren, where are your books?"

Lauren said, "Buh."

"Is the blue one your book?"

She said "buh," again, so I knew she wanted to talk to me.

"Walking is hard for Lauren, too," said Mr. Mistretta. "How old were you when you learned to walk?"

"Almost a year."

"Well, Lauren was three. Her muscles aren't strong. She still walks slowly. Her hands shake too, so it is hard for her to make her letters."

"I can help her walk fast. It's not hard. Look Lauren, follow me." I walked really fast across the room. Lauren just watched.

Next I wondered, "Can she play ball?"

"Try it," said Mr. Mistretta. "People with Down syndrome are all different. Some have a hard time because their muscles aren't strong, but some win Special Olympics playing ball. Roll it to her and see."

"Watch, Lauren," I called. "Catch!" Lauren smiled at me, but she just let the ball roll right past her.

"It takes time," said Mr. Mistretta. "Keep trying. Roll the ball to her even if she misses. Keep asking her questions even if she can't answer yet. After a while she will do more."

The next day I sat with her again. I said, "Lauren, I read about turtles. Have you seen a turtle?" She nodded. "Do you like football? What did you play today?" She smiled. She even made sounds, but I couldn't understand. This was hard. I didn't know if I could help.

Every day I talked to her. I asked questions. I showed her pictures. I told her what I was doing.

Then at Christmas I said, "Look, I drew Santa Claus." Lauren touched my picture. She said, "Ho Ho!" I laughed then, and so did she. That was fun. After that, I drew lots of great pictures for her.

One day Mr. Mistretta asked me to take a note to the office. Lauren wanted to go, too. Mr. Mistretta said, "Take her with you, but go slowly. Practice will help her muscles grow strong."

We started off, but Lauren was way behind me. I waited and she caught up. When I forgot and walked faster, she got behind again. I said, "Hurry up, Lauren," but she didn't hurry up. Finally I just walked very slowly, and she stayed right beside me. It was nice to have a friend to walk with.

When the weather grew warm in the spring, I tried to teach her to play ball. I rolled it to her and yelled, "Catch!" Lauren didn't look, and she missed the ball. I kept trying. Lauren missed again and again, and I had to run and get it every time.

"I'm tired of this, Mr. Mistretta. She always misses."

"Try the jingle ball. The red color and the sound will help her remember."

It helped. Sometimes, she caught it. I felt proud.

Then she did something new. After she caught it, Lauren wanted to hold the ball. She liked to hear it jingle. She wouldn't roll it back, so I still had to go get it.

One day when the school year was almost over, I saw Lauren coming out of our room. "Where's your book?" I asked.

Lauren answered, "Book here."

"Way to go, Lauren," I cheered. You said `book.'" She laughed out loud.

After that we walked a little and sat down. I rolled the big soccer ball to her. This time she watched it, and she caught it. Then she rolled it right back.

"All right, Lauren," I yelled. We were excited.

When Mr. Mistretta saw her, he was excited, too. He called Lauren's Mom and Dad and told them about the new things I helped her learn.

The very next day Lauren's Mom and Dad brought ice cream to school for her and all the peer buddies.

The way I helped her, I could be a good peer buddy for any kid. I hope I can be a peer buddy next year.

DISCUSSION:

¤ What could you do to teach someone with a disability to play a game with you?

¤ How do you think Lauren felt when people couldn't understand her?

¤ If a person doesn't talk to you, how can you help that person?

THE CHAMPIONS
By
Nan Holcomb

Abby looked out her window and watched the moving van pull away from the house next door. She could hardly wait to meet the people who had moved in. Her mother had told her there was a little girl just her age. That was so exciting! Boys had lived there before. They had been her brothers' friends. Now she would have a special friend to do things with.

"Come along, Abby," her mother called. "You can help carry the picnic supper over to our new neighbors."

"Coming!" Abby yelled and ran downstairs. She held out her arms and her mother gave her the box with paper dishes, cloth, plastic knives, forks and spoons. Together they crossed the driveway and rang the bell. Mr. Stevens answered.

"Look, Mary!" he called "The moving-in-day fairies are here with our dinner."

Abby and Mom carried the boxes to the kitchen. Abby turned toward the table and nearly dropped her box. There sat a little girl in a wheelchair.

Mr. Stevens knelt down beside the chair. "Meet your new neighbor, Tina. She has brought us our first dinner in our new home!"

Tina smiled, but Abby backed away from the chair.

"Tina will be in your class in school, Abby," her mother said. "She might also like to go to Brownie Girl Scouts with you."

Abby smiled politely but thought, I don't think so.

At school the next few days, Abby noticed that the other children left Tina alone. Tina didn't look as happy as she had on moving-in day. Abby could guess why. She knew she had walked the long way around the room so she wouldn't have to walk past Tina's chair. She knew she had looked the other way when she felt Tina looking at her. She knew she had not included her in any activities. She knew she hadn't chosen to sit at Tina's table in the lunch room.

Maybe I should invite her to Brownies after all, she thought. Maybe, yes! Maybe, it's a good idea. Her mother thought it was a very good idea and called Tina's mother.

"We'd certainly enjoy visiting," Mrs. Stevens answered.

Boy, Abby thought, this may be a big mistake. She can't really do anything. She just sits in that stupid wheelchair and smiles, and she doesn't even smile much anymore.

When they got to Brownies the girls were already busy in small groups, but Mrs. Larsen called them together to introduce Tina.

"This should be interesting," Abby muttered. Everyone had been walking around Tina and ignoring her for a week. Abby watched their expressions as they all gathered together. Some said "Hi," quietly and looked at the floor or the back of the chair. Some didn't say anything. Abby felt ashamed for them all, but Mrs. Larsen just talked on like everything was normal.

"Now that we're all together we'll just stay together," Mrs. Larsen said. Today we're going on a look-and-see hunt in the back yard. We're going to go with our partners to look for things in our ecology hunt for our Try-it patch. We'll find them and then write them down. We'll look for 3 kinds of leaves, 3 kinds of rocks, 3 kinds of plants, 3 kinds of insects..."

"Wait a minute, Mrs. Larsen," Tammy said. "How can Tina do that? She can't write. She can't even walk around to look."

Abby looked at Tina and felt terrible. Tina's smile had gone. She looked so sad.

"I don't see any problem," Abby said and scowled at Tammy. "*I* will push her chair! Besides, she has very good eyes. She can look and find the different things and I will write them down. No problem!"

"That sounds like a very good way to do it, Abby. I'm sure you'll have a great hunt. Now let's get started, girls. See how many things you can find before I blow this whistle," Mrs. Larsen said.

Abby had never pushed a wheelchair before, but she certainly wasn't going to let anybody know it. Mrs. Stevens and Mom were talking to Mrs. Larsen. "Well, Tina, I guess we'll just do it. Scream if it gets too scary!" Abby said and pushed the chair. It didn't move.

Tina laughed and bounced up and down. She tried to move her hand down and looked down. Abby looked down at the wheel.

"Boy, am I dumb!" she said. "We aren't going anyplace with the brake on!" Tina laughed again.

This time when Abby pushed the chair it began to roll—fast! Tina laughed and waved her arms!

"Hey, this is fun and you're a good sport, Tina," Abby said. Tina waved her arm again and pointed to a tree beside the path. "Good job, Tina. That's two kinds of leaves and two bugs right there!" By the time Abby had them written down, Tina had spotted a pile of rocks. It seemed like no time at all before they heard the whistle.

When everyone returned, guess which team had found 3 kinds of leaves, 3 kinds of rocks, 3 kinds of plants, 3 kinds of bugs and 3 kinds of everything else on the Try-it list? That's right! The team with Tina and Abby were the champions!

Abby looked at Tina's big smile and grinned. " I guess we're two of the best Brownie Girl Scouts in town!" she said and pushed her new best friend over to the snack table.

POLKA DOT BIRTHDAY MAP
By
Kathy Kennedy Tapp

"I hate soup." Kelly pushed her bowl away. She wanted to be home eating cake, not sitting in the school cafeteria on her birthday.

"Aren't you going to eat?" asked Caitlin.

"I hate tomato soup," said Kelly. She didn't know Caitlin very well. She didn't know any of the kids in the special class.

The bell rang.

"Time for class." Caitlin picked up her cane.

Kelly made a face. "I hate this class," she mumbled. She like her other classes where she didn't have to read stupid Braille dots. She grabbed her cane and jabbed it back and forth down the blurry hall full of kids. *They* didn't have to have canes or special classes.

"Happy birthday, Kelly," her teacher, Mrs. White greeted her.

"I didn't know it was your birthday!" Caitlin cried. "Why didn't you tell me?"

"Happy birthday," Steve and Heidi called from across the room.

"I have something special planned for today,"said Mrs. White. She handed Kelly a piece of paper. "For the birthday girl."

"What does it say?" Steve rolled his wheelchair closer.

"I don't know," said Kelly, feeling the dots on the paper. She didn't want to read Braille on her birthday. She gave the paper to Caitlin. "You read it."

Caitlin read out loud.

"A treasure hunt is lots of fun.
The wheelchair swing holds clue #1."

"Outside!" cried Steve excitedly. "The playground."

He led the way, rolling over to the swing that was like a big wooden box for kids in wheelchairs. "I found the clue!" he cried.

"Let Kelly read it," Mrs. White said. "It's her birthday."

Kelly felt the bumps on the paper. She couldn't read Braille as well as Caitlin, but she new some of the letters.

Polka dot map. Poke-a-dot. Would she be able to read the clue?

"It says, 'Go to where...'" She shook her head. "I need help."

Caitlin took the paper. She read slowly:

"Go to where the pine trees grow.
You're doing fine.
Not far to go."

"Pine trees?" Kelly frowned.

"On the front lawn," said Heidi. "They have Christmas lights on them in

82

winter, remember?" she grabbed Kelly's hand. "Come on. I'll show you." Heidi could see better than Kelly and Caitlin. She didn't need a cane, just thick glasses.

Kelly felt the wind blowing her hair, as they ran across the lawn. "Hey, I like this game."

Steve's wheelchair rolled behind them.

"Too many trees. No fair!" Heidi complained.

"That's the fun of it," Mrs. White said. "You have to find the right tree."

Kelly crawled under a big pine tree. She smelled the pine smell and felt the scratchy needles on her head and the bumpy ground under her knees. But she didn't find any Braille paper.

She crawled back out and stood up.

Where were the other kids? Which way was she facing? Did the other kids leave her? The yard was a foggy blur of shapes and shadows.

"Did anyone find it yet?" Steve called. Kelly turned toward his voice.

"No," said Caitlin. "And my hair's full of pine needles."

Kelly breathed a sigh of relief. The other kids were here. She wasn't lost.

"Hey, what about this big tree?" Caitlin cried. "Let's look here, Kelly."

Kelly knelt by the lowest branches and brushed her hand across the prickly needles. She felt something wooden--a clothespin. And something stiff--Braille paper!

"I found it!" she yelled. She touched the dots. Maybe she could read this one herself.

> *"Lots of tables. Lots of chairs.*
> *Birthday treats are there."*

"The cafeteria!" Heidi and Caitlin cried.

"Treats!" yelled Steve. "Let's go!"

"Careful!" Mrs. White called. "Other kids are in class. You have to be quiet."

"I wonder what the treat will be? whispered Caitlin as she and Kelly tapped their canes on the sidewalk. They turned left toward the cafeteria.

"There it is!" cried Heidi. She pulled Kelly over to a table. "Birthday cupcakes!"

"Yours has a candle," Mrs. White said, lighting the candle. "Okay, make a wish, Kelly."

Kelly touched her cupcake. She licked her finger and tasted the frosting. Chocolate. Her favorite. What should she wish for?

Then she grinned. "A treasure hunt," she said. "I want one again next year, with all my friends, like today!"

"Happy Birthday to Kelly," everyone sang.

Kelly took a big breath and blew out the candle.

FOR MORE INFORMATION

UNITED CEREBRAL PALSY ASSOCIATION
1600 L ST #700
WASHINGTON, DC 20036
(800)872-5827

NATIONAL DOWN SYNDROME CONGRESS
1605 CHANTILLY DR, STE 250
ATLANTA, GA 30324
(800)232-6372

AMERICAN SOCIETY FOR DEAF CHILDREN
814 THAYER AVE
SILVER SPRING, MD 20910
(800)942-2732

NATIONAL ASSOCIATION FOR THE DEAF
814 THAYER AVE
SILVER SPRING, MD 20910-4500
(FAX) (301)587-1791

SPINA BIFIDA ASSOCIATION OF AMERICA
4590 MAC ARTHUR BLVD NW #250
WASHINGTON, DC 20007-4226
(800)621-3141

THE AMERICAN COUNCIL OF THE BLIND
1155 15TH ST NW STE 720
WASHINGTON, DC 20005
(202) 467-5081

THE NATIONAL FEDERATION OF THE BLIND
1800 JOHNSON ST
BALTIMORE, MD 21230
(410)659-9314

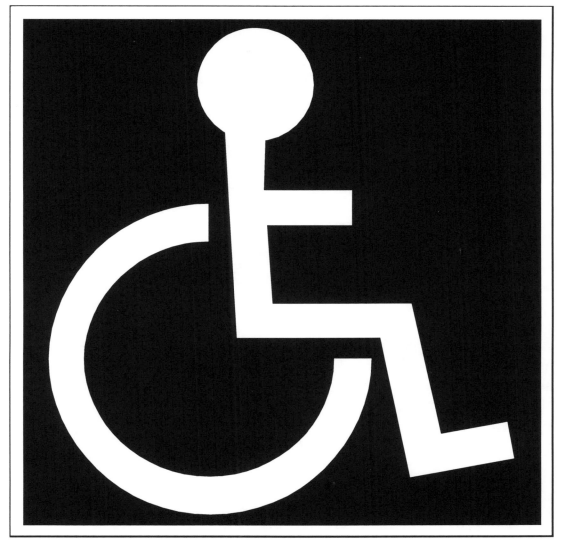

Look for this sign this week.
Circle the places where you have seen this sign.

On the street   At the mall   In the store

At the post office   Other places_____

Can you make the sign for 'cookie'?

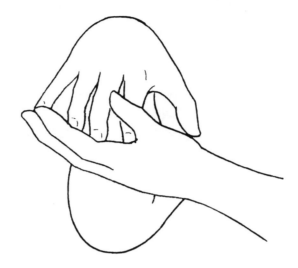

Can you make the sign for 'juice'?

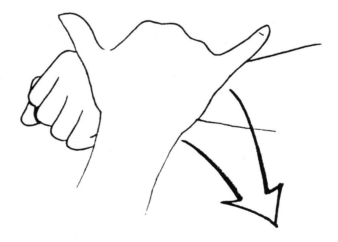

That's right! Good job!

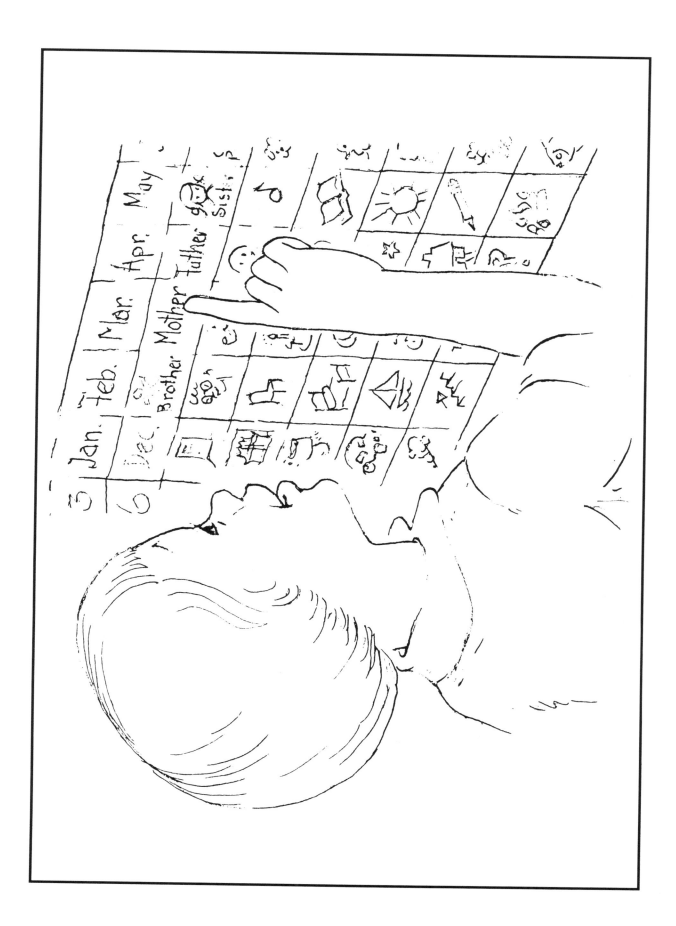

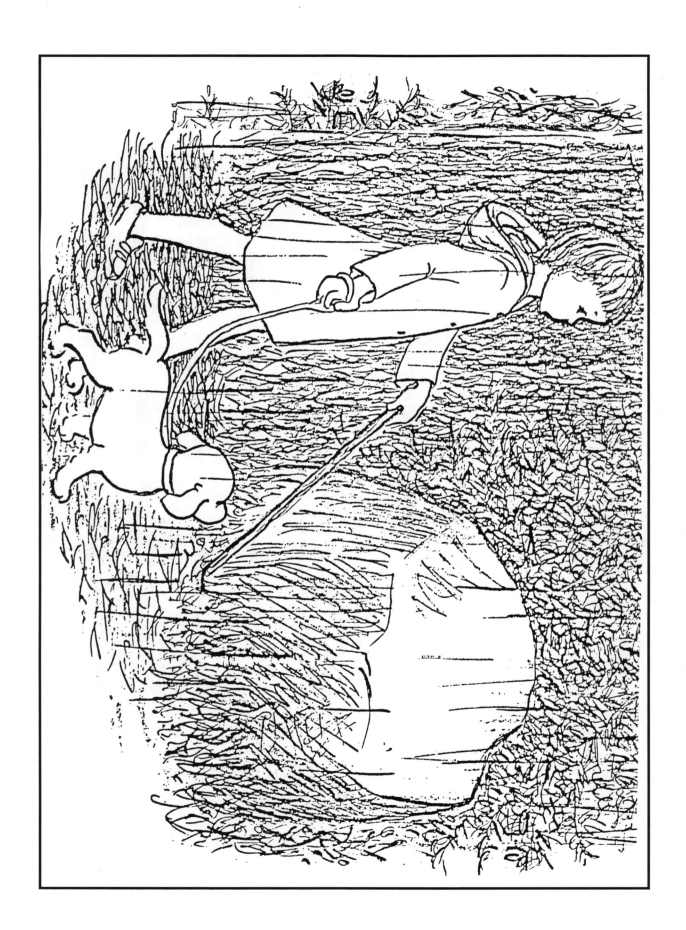